Doing the Right Thing

A Real Estate Practitioner's Guide to Ethical Decision Making

THIRD EDITION

Deborah H. Long

Gorsuch/Prentice Hall

Upper Saddle River, New Jersey 07458

Library of Congress Cataloging-in-Publication Data

Long, Deborah, H.
    Doing the right thing : a real estate practitioner's guide to ethical decision making /
Deborah H. Long.—3rd ed.
      p. cm.
    Includes bibliographical references and index.
    ISBN 0-13-085958-3
    1. Real estate agents—professional ethics. 2. Real estate business—Moral and ethical
aspects. 3. Real estate agents—Professional ethics—Case studies. 4. Real estate
business—Moral and ethical aspects—Case studies. I. Title.

HD1382 .L66 2000
174'.9333—dc21

                                                 00-035375

To my husband, Courtney, the most honest person I know,
and our daughter Jennifer, who reminds me that I have to be a role model.

Acquisitions Editor: Neil Marquardt
Managing Editor: Mary Carnis
Production: Holcomb Hathaway, Inc.
Production Liason: Brian Hyland
Director of Manufacturing and Production: Bruce Johnson
Manufacturing Manager: Ed O'Dougherty
Editorial Assistant: Delia Uherec
Marketing Manager: Shannon Simonsen
Marketing Assistant: Adam Kloza

Prentice-Hall International (UK) Limited, *London*
Prentice-Hall of Australia Pty. Limited, *Sydney*
Prentice-Hall Canada Inc., *Toronto*
Prentice-Hall Hispanoamericana, S.A., *Mexico*
Prentice-Hall of India Private Limited, *New Delhi*
Prentice-Hall of Japan, Inc., *Tokyo*
Pearson Education Singapore Pte. Ltd.
Editora Prentice-Hall do Brasil, Ltda., *Rio de Janeiro*

10 9 8 7 6 5 4 3 2 1
ISBN 0-13-085958-3

Contents

Preface v

1 Ethics and the Practice of Real Estate 1

2 Values, Principles, and Ethics 7
Understanding Principles and Values 7
Where Our Values Come From 12
Developing a Personal Code of Ethics 15

3 The Evolution of Moral Reasoning 19

4 Ethical Systems 27
End-Results Ethics 28
Rule or Law Ethics 31
Social Contract Ethics 32
Transformational Ethics 35

5 Models for Ethical Decision Making 39
The Kew Gardens Principle 45
A Rational Model of Ethical Analysis 49
Rotarian Model for Ethical Decision Making 52

6 Professional Perspectives 53
Professional Practice Standards 55
Reasonable Person Standard 56
Ethics and the Law 57

7 **Applying Ethics: Agency   61**

Differences Between Clients and Customers   62

Agency and Non-Agency Relationships   63

Lawsuits Concerning Agency Representation   65

How Would You Respond?   68

Possible Responses   71

8 **Applying Ethics: Fair Housing   77**

How Would You Respond?   82

Possible Responses   86

9 **Applying Ethics: Stigmatized Property   93**

How Would You Respond?   96

Possible Responses   97

10 **Applying Ethics: Environmental Hazards and Other Physical Defects   99**

Radon Gas   101

Lead-Based Paint   102

Seller Disclosure   104

How Would You Respond?   106

Possible Responses   107

11 **Applying Ethics: Working with Colleagues and Employers   111**

How Would You Respond?   118

Possible Responses   120

12 **Applying Ethics: Community and Public Concerns   123**

How Would You Respond?   126

Possible Responses   128

A Closing Note   130

Appendix: Resources for More Information   131

References   133

Index   135

Preface

The perception of real estate practitioners as unethical is so commonplace that the term *real estate ethics* is considered an oxymoron by members of the public and often by the profession itself! Negative characterizations appear everywhere in the popular media; witness, for example, the portrayal of real estate agents in such films as *Glengarry Glen Ross, Pacific Heights,* and *Wall Street.*

Real estate practitioners are no more or less ethical than the average American. However, we often have a difficult time doing the right thing for a few reasons: first, confusing, complex, and sometimes contradictory laws, rules, and codes of conduct govern real estate practitioners; and second, practitioners lack decision-making experience confronting ethical dilemmas.

This book was designed to help real estate practitioners face and resolve these problems. The objectives of this guide are fourfold: to help real estate practitioners (1) become aware of personal values and principles; (2) formulate a personal code of ethics; (3) become aware of laws and regulations (or the lack thereof) that may govern responses to ethical dilemmas; and (4) develop and implement a rational model for ethical decision making.

The text is written in workbook format so that readers can respond to the exercises individually or as part of a class exercise. To keep the discussion grounded in reality, case studies from real estate trade magazines and journals, as well as from daily newspapers, appear in the chapters.

The first half of the book, Chapters 1–6, provides background to the problems that confront real estate professionals and insight into the development of values, principles, and ethics. These chapters also introduce a philosophical and psychological overview of moral development so that readers can better understand their own methods for resolving ethical dilemmas. Models for ethical decision making are provided to enable readers to employ a variety of strategies for dealing with ethical problems in real estate. Finally, readers are given some guidance on professional and legal standards governing the real estate business.

The second half of the book, Chapters 7–12, is a handbook and a workbook. These chapters examine specific ethical issues, such as agency, civil rights, stigmatized properties, environmental hazards, and relationships with colleagues, employers, and the community. Each chapter ends with questions ("How Would You Respond?") and possible responses dealing with dilemmas commonly confronted by real estate practitioners. Lastly, a list of additional resources is provided for readers who wish to explore ethical issues not only in real estate, but in business generally and at home.

Today's real estate practitioners are more likely to encounter difficult ethical issues than ever before. Like professionals everywhere, real estate agents can choose to engage in responsible and morally desirable behavior, help people in need, and do the right thing. This book points us in that direction.

Acknowledgments

I was fortunate to be surrounded by supportive family, colleagues, friends, and mentors during the writing of this book. Without my husband's encouragement and willingness to take on more than his share of family responsibility, I would never have been able to complete my work on time. Our daughter, Jennifer, should be commended for her patience while I spent hours at the word processor. I promise to make it up to her. I also wish to acknowledge the influence of my sister and mother, my friends, and my graduate professors in the shaping of this work. I am particularly grateful to the following real estate educators, who reviewed the original manuscript and offered suggestions as to how it might be improved: Richard J. Clemmer, Hugh Ryall, Leslie Campbell, Barry Caudill, Charles E. Krackeler, and John Reilly. My colleagues Richard Linkemer, Maryann Bassett, and Cindy Chandler, my students, and numerous state regulators have contributed their ideas to this new edition. I also wish to thank colleagues who provided me with the news clippings referred to in the new case studies.

I became interested in this project for a number of reasons. When people discover that I teach basic licensing law and principles to real estate practitioners, they often relate stories of real or perceived poor ethical conduct by practitioners with whom they have come in contact. As an educator, I became interested in whether ethical reasoning skills could be taught in a classroom to adults whose reasoning skills and moral conduct have already been shaped by earlier influences. My graduate work indicates that ethics education can make a difference in the way we think and act.

Perhaps more significantly, I am a child of Holocaust survivors, and as such, I have always been disturbed by the fact that the horrors of Auschwitz and Nazi Germany were perpetrated by educated people: architects and engineers built the crematoria; medical doctors performed inhumane experiments on victims; and lawyers made it legal. The many moral failures witnessed in the Holocaust can ultimately be attributed to a system that valued many things over the development of character and conscience. All of the skills we acquire in the classroom and at work are meaningless unless we are taught the value of human life: without ethical reasoning skills, we are not fully human.

Deborah Long

Ethics and the Practice of Real Estate

> *Meno:* Can you tell me, Socrates, whether virtue is acquired by teaching or by practice; or if neither by teaching nor practice, then whether it comes to man by nature, or in what other way?
>
> *Socrates:* You must think I am very fortunate to know how virtue is acquired. The fact is that far from knowing whether it can be taught, I have no idea what virtue is.

Never has it been more difficult to be a real estate agent than it is today. Not only are real estate professionals grappling with significant technological changes in the industry, they are dealing with social and cultural upheaval as well. In the last 15 years, technological innovations such as the Internet, personal computers, fax machines, and cellular telephones have given practitioners faster access to more information. These marvelous inventions have revolutionized the brokerage business and changed the way agents handle their day-to-day business.

Social changes have also transformed the real estate marketplace. In the last few decades, the U.S. economy has shifted from an industrial to a service orientation. Baby-boomers are aging, women are participating in the workforce in greater numbers, and the number of single-parent households is rising. These demographic changes have had an enormous impact on the real estate marketplace. They also provide opportunities—if we are prepared for them. New technology means we can provide our customers and clients with more information faster. Social and cultural changes can lead to new markets for residential and commercial real estate.

1

Social, demographic, and technological change—particularly rapid change—can be challenging and stressful. If new technology creates faster access to more information, it also demands higher education and more critical thinking skills for professionals. While real estate practitioners once were considered mere conduits of information, practitioners today must interpret and evaluate information, not merely pass it along. In the area of finance, for example, brokers and salespersons have to keep up-to-date on almost a minute-by-minute basis to discuss the advantages and disadvantages of various loan programs intelligently.

Information about real estate is more accessible than ever to the public. Today's buyers and sellers demand competence and accountability from their real estate agents. They ask more and tougher questions about issues that were not in our vocabulary 15 years ago: radon, electromagnetic fields (EMFs), and lead-based paint, to name a few.

Social and demographic changes can open up new markets, but in order to serve those markets, real estate professionals must also adapt. To best serve all their clients, agents today may benefit from being bi- or multi-lingual and from understanding how to deal with individuals from various cultures. Agents must also be sensitive to gender, race, and disability issues. In addition to the demands of a dynamic marketplace, real estate agents must understand constantly changing federal, state, and local laws.

The demands upon real estate professionals to meet these day-to-day challenges are overwhelming. While pre- and post-licensing courses provide real estate students with the information about practices, principles, and state laws needed to enter the profession, rarely do these courses supply the skills necessary for *survival* in the business. It is no surprise, then, that practitioners are not always up to the challenge. According to the Association of Real Estate License Law Officials, in 1997 alone, state regulatory agencies investigated over 28,000 complaints against real estate agents and over 3,800 real estate agents in the U.S. and Canada lost their licenses, either through suspension or revocation, or paid an administrative fine. Since candidates must undergo a background check before licensure, it may be safe to assume that few of these complaints were filed against individuals who had *criminal* intent to harm the public. Any of three additional assumptions may be made:

1. Many of these agents got "in trouble" not because they had criminal tendencies, but because they either were unaware of or did not fully understand the rules, regulations, and/or laws they violated.

2. The offenders, though not career criminals, were *aware* of the rules, regulations, and laws and violated them knowingly.

3. They were aware of the rules and laws but *poor judgment* caused them to make bad decisions regarding their professional behavior.

Many believe that once we become adults, our values, principles, and behavior are set in stone. In fact, some believe that these are firmly established by the age of five. Both beliefs are myths. If they were true, we would have to relinquish all hope that education and experience have any power to change us.

The belief that change is possible is not merely wishful thinking. Psychologists and educational researchers have provided significant evidence that experience and education can improve the ability to reason morally. However, these studies indicate that for ethics education to be effective—that is, for individuals to become more ethical—several conditions must exist. First, we must be exposed to ethical philosophies and ideas. We also need a chance to explore our own values and principles before going on to role play and internalize ethical teaching. Finally, for an ethics program to be valuable and sustainable, we must be exposed to individuals who reason at higher levels.

Unfortunately, *having* an enhanced ability to reason morally does not necessarily translate to *using* it. Ethics instruction can remove moral blinders, make us more aware of moral values, and enhance self-knowledge and decision-making ability, but without the support of caring parents, friends, coworkers, and society, it is difficult to nurture a conscience. Knowing what is ethical is no guarantee of ethical behavior.

What makes people do the right thing? Moral action comes from competence, will, and habit. Psychologist Thomas Lickona (1992) argues that *moral competence* is the ability to turn moral judgment and feeling into effective moral action. He defines will as a "mobilizing of energy to do what we think we should" (p. 62). Habit results from the practice of being a good person so that doing the right thing becomes an unconscious practice.

What stops us from doing the right thing? Sometimes we lack the ability to deal with an ethical issue (competence), cannot resist temptation and withstand peer pressure (will), or have little practice at being good (habit). Other times, our own misplaced beliefs about ethics prevent us from acting.

Consider the following myths and the corresponding realistic views concerning them.

MYTH	REALITY
In order to make an ethical decision, we must be morally perfect.	Even exceptionally good people make poor moral judgments or commit unethical acts. Developing character is not a short-term process but a lifelong one.
Ethical behavior is based on values and one person's values are as good as another's.	This type of thinking, called moral relativism, teaches that any judgment that reins in personal freedom is intolerable. However, we must measure values against a standard, otherwise we cannot distinguish between what we want to do and what we should do.

The answers to all ethical problems can be found in our professional code of ethics.

Codes structure an understanding of behavior, but they rarely anticipate every problem that we may face.

Making ethical decisions means playing God. It's not up to me to make these decisions.

In most ethical dilemmas, you can rely on rules, policies, and laws that lead you to reasonable solutions. In other cases, you must search your soul or conscience. Some believe conscience is the divine spark within. Remember, not making a decision has consequences, just as taking action does. You are not powerless to act. Govern yourself accordingly.

People are either ethical or not.

Everyone is capable of a variety of responses to ethical dilemmas ranging from inappropriate to appropriate, from wrong to right, from illegal to legal. Whether people behave ethically or not depends upon the circumstances at that moment.

If people would just follow the law, we wouldn't have ethical problems.

The law sets a minimum standard for acceptable behavior. Living by ethical standards inspires us to do more than the law requires.

Real estate professionals always know when they are acting unethically.

They often do not know. The ethical dilemmas we confront are so complicated that we need all the resources we have to solve them.

Adults can't change their ethics. It's too late.

Research indicates that adults can improve their ethical thinking skills as well as their conduct. The greatest period of increased ethical consciousness is during the twenties and thirties, when young adults face ethical dilemmas on their own for the first time. Stage development also occurs when adults face a life transition or crisis that forces them to reevaluate their conduct or thinking. Research also indicates that education programs can increase ethical thinking skills.

I'm just one person. What can I do that will make any difference?

Everything you say and everything you do, no matter how insignificant to you, can bear a message or have a consequence. The authors of *Chicken Soup for the Soul* illustrate this by describing a man who was walking along a beach and noticed that, because of the low tide, thousands of starfish were stranded on the beach. A second man was walking toward him picking up starfish and throwing them back into the ocean. The first man asked the second man why he was doing this since he couldn't save all the starfish, and therefore, his actions wouldn't make a difference. The other man responded by picking up another starfish, throwing it back into the water, and saying "Made a difference to that one."

Being ethical is great, but I still have to earn a living and work in the rat race.

Ethics and business are not mutually exclusive. Practical solutions can be ethical, and the pursuit of ethical excellence can yield material rewards. Many firms place a value on loyalty, avoiding harm to others, being just, and earning trust and respect. As comedienne Lily Tomlin once said, "The trouble is even if you win the rat race, you're still a rat."

"I'VE BEEN HEARING DISTURBING RUMORS OF A TAKEOVER BID."

Our misplaced belief in these myths sometimes causes us to exercise poor ethical judgment. Nevertheless, remedies are available: real estate practitioners have access to continuing education courses, professional seminars and workshops, and trade journals. More and more often, state regulatory agencies order violators to attend continuing education courses. Furthermore, the majority of states have mandated that all licensees return to the classroom every few years for an update on evolving laws or practices.

Few education courses exist to help practitioners make good decisions when facing moral or ethical dilemmas. Courses that do help licensees develop their moral reasoning ability compress the information into three hours or fewer! Research indicates that improving an adult's ethical reasoning requires a more sustained educational program.

It has never been more important to learn. In light of the technological, social, and demographic changes sweeping our business, it is increasingly important that we learn to navigate new and uncertain ethical terrain. Learning to make sound ethical judgments is a lifetime task, usually begun in childhood by our parents, elaborated upon by teachers and peers, and never finished. As real estate professionals and concerned individuals, we must begin to understand our own value systems and see how these values aid in dealing with ethical dilemmas.

Values, Principles, and Ethics

Strong personal character should manifest itself in service to organizations and communities and in courage in public life. The moral crisis of our time means more and more people lack the liberating self-mastery that allows them to commit and serve independence and integrity befitting a free people.

Walter Nicgorski

Ethical dilemmas constantly confront the real estate agent. For example, one of the most common dilemmas in real estate is balancing our fiduciary responsibility to our client with the customer's right to know. Disclosing information such as a leaky roof or the possible presence of radon may curtail a buyer's interest. Rather than giving primary consideration to the legal and ethical issues at stake, real estate agents may find their responses tempered by the amount of the commission involved.

How can we recognize when a business decision has ethical implications? Consider the "red flags" listed in the box on page 8. All of these concerns indicate an ethical dilemma, and recognizing a problem is the first step toward resolution. Before we can respond to an ethical dilemma, however, we must understand how we think about moral problems. What are principles, values, and ethics? Often these terms are used interchangeably, but for our purposes, we must distinguish between them.

Understanding Principles and Values

Principles are fundamental truths. They serve as enduring moral guideposts. Similar principles are found across most cultures and religions and provide a guide for human and institutional conduct. Principles are made up

Ethical Dilemmas—Characteristics and Examples

Here are some signals that I am facing an ethical dilemma. When I think about this situation:

- I use words such as "right," "wrong," "bottom line," "values," "conflict of interest," or "ethics."
- I want to call the state regulatory agency (or a local real estate school or professional association hotline) to determine its legality.
- I question whether my actions or inactions will harm anyone. I list the advantages and disadvantages of my decision.
- I question whether I am being fair to everyone. I wonder if I would do the same thing if others were involved. The Golden Rule comes to mind: "Do unto others as you would have them do unto you."
- I feel that something is wrong.
- I feel torn between two or more values, goals, or parties.
- I hesitate to share this problem with others. I worry that others may object to or oppose my decision.
- I worry what others will think about it.

Here are some situations where I might face an ethical dilemma:

- I'm showing a minority couple a neighborhood where there have been incidents of racial unrest. Should I tell the buyers?
- A suspected child molester wants to make an offer on my listing near an elementary school.
- My seller has asked me to conceal the property's proximity to EMFs.
- A suicide took place on this property two months ago. My seller–client does not want me to reveal this information to prospects.
- My broker has asked me to conceal escrow fund shortages.
- My top-producing agent is using drugs. Should I terminate him or try to correct the problem?
- I've rejected a listing because it was in a minority neighborhood that I don't service.
- I've negotiated a contract that will cause environmentally sensitive land to be developed.

of "natural" laws found throughout history. They are permanent, reflect human morals, and carry a great obligation.

Principles are not the same as values, but the two are related. What we value can become the building blocks of our principles. As Stephen R. Covey (1989) wrote in *The Seven Habits of Highly Effective People,* "Principles are the territory. Values are maps. When we value correct principles, we have truth, a knowledge of things as they are" (p. 35).

Examples of Principles

On fairness: "Do unto others as you would have them do unto you." (the Golden Rule)

On self: "To thine own self be true." (Shakespeare)

On freedom: "It is better to die on your feet than live on your knees." (Dolores Ibarruri, Paris, 1936)

---

1. *Values are mutable and temporary.* For example, an older person may value health more than a young person. A person who has lost a relative may prize family more than someone who has not.

2. *Values can be nonmoral or illegal.* For example, someone may value a stolen object or a high-speed drive down the highway.

3. *Values do not necessarily carry a sense of obligation.* Values may merely express likes or dislikes. For example, someone may value jazz as a form of expression but not be obligated to attend a jazz concert.

EXERCISE   Values Auction

Use the following exercise to determine what you value. Imagine that you are attending an auction of values, and you have twenty $10 bills, totalling $200. You must spend the entire $200 to purchase values from the list below, using only $10 increments. You may spend more on one value than on others. Spending more or less on different values indicates how important those values are to you.

$ _____ Accountability   Accepting the consequences of your actions and the responsibility for your decisions. Setting an example for others and avoiding the appearance of impropriety.

$ _____ Caring

Treating people as ends in themselves, not as means to an end. Having compassion; treating people courteously and with dignity; helping those in need; avoiding harm to others.

$ _____ Education

Completing your educational goals with good/outstanding grades.

$ _____ Fairness

Being open-minded and willing to admit error; not taking undue advantage of another; avoiding favoritism; treating people equally and justly.

$ _____ Family

Having a warm, pleasant family life.

$ _____ Freedom

Living in an environment at work and home that maximizes personal freedom and independence.

$ _____ Friendship

Having companions you can count on and forming lasting friendships.

$ _____ Health

Having good health with almost total absence of physical or mental problems.

$ _____ Helping Others

Contributing to the emotional, physical, and educational well-being of others through work or hobbies.

$ _____ High Income

Earning top income early in your career.

$ _____ Honesty/Integrity

Being truthful. Keeping commitments. Being faithful to principles.

$ _____ Leisure

Having free time to enjoy personal pleasures.

$ _____ Loyalty

Being faithful to those with whom you have a relationship, whether in business or in friendship.

$ _____ Justice

Working to preserve the rights of others in society.

$ _____ Moral Courage

Being able to think and do the right thing, even at risk to personal well-being.

$ _____ Prestige

Having status in your community or society due to achievement.

$ _____ Pursuit of Excellence

Striving to be as good as you can be: being industrious, committed, and professional.

$ _____ Respect for   Recognizing each person's right to privacy,
           Others   self-determination, and decision making.
                           Affording others dignity, courtesy, and tol-
                           erance.

$ _____ Responsible   Obeying just laws; safeguarding the demo-
           Citizenship   cratic process.

$ _____ Self   Putting yourself first and knowing when to
                           say no.

Adapted from J. Harris-Bowlsbey, J. D. Spivack, and R. S. Lisansky, 1986. "Values Auction" in *Take Hold of Your Future: Leader's Manual.* Towson, MD: ACT Career Planning Services.

EXERCISE   Analyzing Your Values

Based on your responses to the previous exercise, list in descending order the top 10 values on which you spent the most money (you may not need all 10 spaces):

MOST   VALUE

1. $ _____   _____

2. $ _____   _____

3. $ _____   _____

4. $ _____   _____

5. $ _____   _____

6. $ _____   _____

7. $ _____   _____

8. $ _____   _____

9. $ _____   _____

10. $ _____   _____

LEAST

Consider the monetary value you applied to each of the top 10 items. Are amounts distributed evenly among these 10? Are some values weighted more heavily than others? How do these important values guide your life?

If you had to choose between two important values, which one would take precedence? How do these values interact?

_____

_____

_____

_____

_____

Where Our Values Come From

We should not only consider the relative importance of our values, but we should also question where our values come from and how they are shaped.

Psychologists contend that one of the first and most primary influences upon moral development is parents. Numerous studies of parent–infant relationships have confirmed that the first year of life is critical in human development. Babies who are secure in their parents' love grow up to be independent and to form positive, healthy relationships with their peers. Their sense of security allows them to stand on their own feet in times of moral crisis. On the other hand, if a positive attachment to a parent figure is not formed during that first year and continued through childhood, normal human relations and moral development may never happen. Individuals who never develop the ability to love and value others often become amoral, as exemplified by the many serious criminal offenders who were starved of normal socialization during their childhoods.

Parents can provide a child with an image of what a good person is and does. If parents are generous, honest, sharing, and loving, those qualities become the "voice inside," the conscience of the developing child. This internal voice is crucial to teenagers who feel the powerful influence of peers on their behavior. Other adults can become important during this period, particularly as models of the work ethic. Role models such as work supervisors can help teens see themselves as productive and able. A positive attitude toward work gives teenagers pride, dignity, and responsibility.

Religion can also act as a primary influence on moral development. Over 94 percent of Americans believe in a supreme deity (*Newsweek,* March 27, 1989). For many, religion guides moral decisions and provides an incentive for leading a moral life. While religions differ on how to achieve moral perfection, most agree that the way we deal with our moral choices affects the quality of our lives both here and after.

Schoolteachers can offer moral guidance by teaching about values through the curriculum. Although public education still wrestles with the appropriateness of values education, educators who provide examples of heroism, patriotism, honesty, and other values through literature and history teach the importance of principles. Children are also taught values through the example of their teachers. Teachers who are fair and loving provide one model; teachers who are prejudiced and unloving provide another. Too many adults have learned negative values from their teachers: compliance to witless rules, learning without joy, and gaining knowledge without character. Fortunately, many adults have also been inspired by their teachers. Good teachers help give us self-esteem to make the hard choices of adulthood.

Cheating in College

In a survey conducted by Rutgers University of 15,000 students at 31 universities, 87 percent of business majors said they had cheated at least once on a test during college. Humanities majors admitted to cheating the least—67 percent. (From the Ethics Resource Center *Ethics Journal*. Reported in the *Palm Beach Post*, 27 September 1993, p. 3.)

In June, 1999, twenty-five San Diego State University students got an "F" for cheating in their ethics class. About one-third of those enrolled in a business ethics course were caught using answers to a quiz. All were given failing grades for the course and most were placed on probation. (From the San Diego State University student newspaper, *The Daily Aztec*, June 18, 1999, p. 1.)

We also learn about moral conduct from leaders, whether from business, entertainment, government, or sports. Former President Jimmy Carter's involvement in Habitat for Humanity, an organization dedicated to sheltering the homeless, Paul Newman's activism on behalf of critically ill children, Mother Teresa's work with impoverished children, and Princess Diana's involvement in land mine removal are just a few examples of moral leadership.

The media can also be an effective teacher of morality. The cinema and theater offer provocative insight into the nature of moral decisions. Unforgettable characters such as those portrayed in *Serpico, Schindler's List,* and *A Man for All Seasons* teach us that sacrifices are sometimes necessary when confronting an ethical dilemma. These films contain very human characters with personality flaws who ultimately triumph and demonstrate moral courage.

One of the most important influences on values is our friends. We are especially vulnerable to our peers and their value systems in our teen years, when our self-esteem and worth largely depend on the opinions of others. As teens, we are often torn between rebelling against parental values and identifying with our peers. Until we learn the value of independent thinking and the relative worth of popularity, our friends may sometimes be the most influential—but not necessarily the best—source of values.

Culture is also an excellent conduit of values. For example, Americans are generally thought of as valuing individualism, a pioneering spirit, entrepreneurism, and material goods. Asians are frequently characterized as prizing solitude, spirituality, and education. Cultures often transmit values based on gender: many cultures value passivity and dependence in women and assertiveness and independence in men. Although such characterizations often lead to stereotyping, they can also provide insight into the influence of culture on value systems.

Thus, parents, religion, teachers, leaders, the media, and culture all affect our moral development and contribute to our values and principles.

EXERCISE   Assessing Sources of Values

Review your top 10 list of values. From whom or what did you gain these values?

Choose five from your list and try to pinpoint the source of those particular values and think about how they were transmitted to you.

Value _____   Source _____

Value _____   Source _____

Value _____   Source _____

Value _____   Source _____

Value _____   Source _____

Is there a main source for many of your values, an overriding influence? If so, who or what? Why?

_____

_____

_____

_____

_____

Developing a Personal Code of Ethics

Once you are aware of your deepest values, you can consider the fundamental principles that ground your values. Ideally, these principles guide your life, give you an identity and self-esteem, and empower you. Your personal environment may change daily, but with these principles you have an unchanging personal constitution that allows you to act in a manner consistent with your values.

If you are true to your principles, and if these principles are founded on worthwhile values, you act as an ethical individual. *Ethics are the methods by which you implement your principles.* Ethics are the system through which you act upon and act out your deepest convictions and do the right thing.

Review the illustration below. Many individuals *feel* strongly about the value of fairness. This emotional commitment is implemented in their *belief* in principle of the Golden Rule, "Do unto others as you would have them do unto you." The implementation of this principle is borne out by their conduct or *actions*. An ethical individual will be consistent in feelings, thoughts, and actions.

A personal code of ethics governs our personal and business relationships. If we integrate our values and principles into a code of conduct, our behavior becomes consistent and mature, offering guidance and inspiration

| Figure 2.1 | The relationship of values, principles, and ethics. |

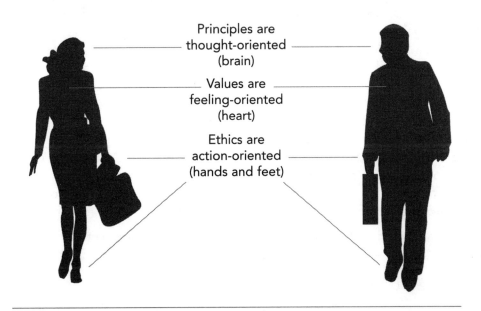

Principles are
thought-oriented
(brain)

Values are
feeling-oriented
(heart)

Ethics are
action-oriented
(hands and feet)

for others. Because real estate practitioners work in a competitive environment where negotiation and persuasion are central, a code of ethics can provide leadership and guidance. Thus, ethics are vital to our success as real estate practitioners, as wives and husbands, as parents, as friends, and ultimately, as human beings.

The Right Way and the Strong Way   *by Joe Murray**

The funeral notice in the newspaper said Kenneth Crain was maintenance supervisor for a rural school district, was born in Angelina County on October 1, 1933, received two Purple Hearts in Korea, and was a former city councilman. I just wish there had been space to tell the story of how he singlehandedly brought civil rights reform to the local union hall.

This happened back in the early 1960s. Though the membership was all male, there were two restrooms in the union hall. One had a sign that said "White." The other had a sign that said "Colored."

Kenneth Crain was a good union man. Moreover, he was a good man, with a strong sense of right and wrong. He had served with blacks in the military, he had worked with blacks on the job, and he lived in a part of town where blacks were his neighbors.

He loved the union. He hated those signs.

Kenneth Crain, too, loved what America stood for. He believed in his country, and he believed in democracy. When something was wrong—when it needed to be changed, and somebody had to do something about it—the right was the American way. You discussed the problem, you debated the issues, and then you took a vote. In the end, right won out. That was what America stood for.

That's what Kenneth Crain did.

He brought the problem of "White" and "Colored" restrooms to the attention of the union leadership. Maybe they didn't see it as a problem, but maybe they hadn't taken the time to think about it.

Kenneth Crain debated the issues with anyone who would listen. He spoke his mind and made his voice heard. He said it was wrong, it ought to be changed, somebody ought to do something about it. Finally, thanks to the prodding of Kenneth Crain, the issue was brought to a vote before the full membership. The men of the various unions came together as one body, to meet, to consider and to vote their conscience. *(continued)*

*Joe Murray is editor and publisher of the Lufkin Daily News *and senior writer for Cox Newspapers.*

The Right Way and the Strong Way   Continued.

This was democracy in action. This was the American way. The will of the majority would not be denied. So they voted. They voted by a 2-1 margin to keep the restrooms the way they were, the way they'd always been, "White" and "Colored," separate but equal.

The majority had spoken, and Kenneth Crain didn't have anything else to say about it. Instead, he just did something about it.

He got up from his seat, went over to the restrooms and singlehandedly ripped the "Colored" sign from the wall and smashed it into splinters. Then he announced to his union brethren that he'd stomp the hell out of any man who tried to put that sign back up.

Kenneth Crain had a strong sense of right and wrong. He also had a strong right. There was no further discussion, no additional debate. The vote carried—one man, one vote.

After that, the union put two other signs on the restrooms. Both signs said the same thing. Both said "Men."

From J. Murray, *The Right Way and the Strong Way.* © 1993 by *Lufkin Daily News.* All rights reserved. Reprinted by permission.

Real Estate Agent Saves Home

A Miami, Florida, real estate agent visited elderly homeowners who wished to list their home and discovered that the motivating reason for the sale was that they could not afford to pay the $1,600 property tax due. After hearing the story, agent Christiane Malone decided she couldn't take the listing, and instead asked associates from her firm and other companies to send in donations. Some 48 real estate professionals chipped in, donating enough to pay off the taxes and to make much-needed repairs on the home. A Boy Scout troop agreed to paint the house as well.

From *Florida REALTOR,* June, 1998, p. 34.

The Evolution of
Moral Reasoning

At each higher stage (of moral development), a person is better able to stand in the shoes of others, integrate conflicting perspectives on a moral problem, appreciate the consequences of this or that course of action, and make a decision that respects the rights of all parties.

Thomas Lickona

Though personal values may change over time, principles are habits—or at least, once we are aware of our principles, we should make them habit. This habit of thinking or behaving in a principled way could be called our code of conduct or ethics. *Ethics can be defined as a system of moral behavior based on principles.*

As adults, we establish fairly constant patterns of ethical behavior. We may agonize over social problems such as abortion and euthanasia and change our minds as we age, but the way we think and respond to such issues is remarkably systematized.

Harvard University Professor Lawrence Kohlberg devoted his life to studying the evolution of moral reasoning. His research not only transformed the landscape of moral development theory but also profoundly influenced ethics education. Kohlberg argued that people learn to reason morally and ethically in definite, sequential stages. Cultural or other factors may speed up, slow down, or even arrest the development of moral reasoning in an individual, but the sequence of the various stages cannot be altered.

To validate his theory of moral reasoning, Kohlberg and later researchers developed ethical reasoning tests and examined how people thought about moral dilemmas. One of Kohlberg's most famous questions asked participants to respond to the moral dilemma in the following exercise.

EXERCISE	Heinz's Dilemma

In Europe, a woman was near death from a special kind of cancer. There was one drug that doctors thought might save her. It was a form of radium that a druggist in the same town had recently discovered. The drug was expensive to make, but the druggist was charging 10 times what the drug cost. The sick woman's husband, Heinz, went to everyone he knew to borrow the money, but he could only get together about half of what it cost. He told the druggist that his wife was dying, and asked him to sell it cheaper or let him pay later. But the druggist refused. Heinz is desperate and is thinking about breaking into the man's store to steal the drug for his wife.

Would the husband be justified in stealing? Why or why not? What do you think?

_____

_____

_____

_____

_____

_____

Kohlberg determined that there are six stages of moral reasoning, as illustrated on pages 22–23.

According to Kohlberg, most children under the age of nine, some teenagers, and many adolescent and adult criminal offenders become stuck at Stage 1 or 2. These individuals view rules and social expectation as an external force. Stage 3 and 4 individuals, on the other hand, have internalized the rules and expectations of others, especially authorities, and accept and understand societal rules based on the general underlying moral principles. Sometimes these underlying principles come into conflict with societal rules—at which point an individual at Stage 5 or 6 will base decisions on principle rather than convention. However, only a minority of adults reach this last stage, usually not until after the age of 20.

An individual reasoning at the Stage 1 level might argue, "Heinz should not steal the drug because it is bad to steal. Heinz would be a thief, and he would be punished for the theft." A Stage 1 thinker might also be concerned about punishment if Heinz doesn't steal the drug (for example, perhaps his wife's family would shun him). These responses, typical of Stage 1 thinkers, do not indicate a value for life over property.

A Stage 2 thinker would consider stealing for someone of value, such as a wife. If a mere acquaintance were ill, the man might not steal. A Stage 2 thinker might also reason that if Heinz could get something in return by stealing, that is, a wife who would be around a little longer to cook or clean for him, then stealing the drug might be justifiable. Stage 2 thinkers are primarily concerned with their own needs.

A Stage 3 thinker might argue that people should care for other people because life is more important than material things. The man should risk stealing to save the life of anyone. A person who did not steal under these circumstances would be a bad person. However, a Stage 3 thinker would also be very concerned about what others would think if he stole anything.

A Stage 4 thinker also considers the value of life and deems it important, even sacred. However, at this level of moral reasoning, an individual may feel that a relationship does not obligate one to steal, no matter how that person values life. A Stage 4 thinker might also consider whether the druggist's right to his invention should be respected.

A Stage 5 individual might believe that one is obligated to steal for anyone dying. Moreover, if the law were to punish Heinz for stealing the drug, the law is not a just law and should be broken. A Stage 5 thinker might say, "Heinz's wife's right to life comes before the druggist's right to property." However, Stage 5 thinkers may also reason that stealing is wrong because society would fall apart if everyone stole what they needed.

Where Stage 5 individuals might ask, "What does it mean to be a good member of my social system? What are my responsibilities to other members of my system?" a Stage 6 thinker would consider, "What does it mean to be a human being? What are my responsibilities to any other human being, even people who do not belong to my system?" Where a Stage 5 person might ask, "Does this action promote my social system?" a Stage 6 person would ask, "Does this action respect the rights of the individual people affected?"

A Stage 6 thinker would act to demonstrate the greatest possible respect for the human rights of everyone and to support a social system that protects those rights. Standing outside of their own social system, Stage 6 thinkers can evaluate the morality of the system and use the principle of respect for others to guide their actions.

Kohlberg described higher levels of reasoning, but he was not judgmental. Heinz's Dilemma has no right or wrong answer. What Kohlberg

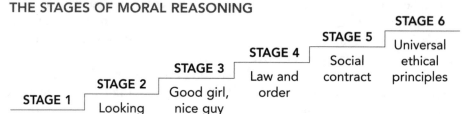

| Figure 3.1 | Kohlberg's summary of moral reasoning. |

THE STAGES OF MORAL REASONING

STAGE 1   *Might makes right.*

Obedience to authority in order to avoid punishment is the most important value.

What's right: I should do what I am told.

Why: To stay out of trouble.

STAGE 2   *Looking out for number one.*

Each person takes care of him- or herself. The only reason to be nice to others is so they will be nice to you.

What's right: I should look out for myself and only be nice to those who are nice to me.

Why: Self-interest.

STAGE 3   *Good girl, nice guy.*

Being good is pleasing to other people and wins their praise. Approval is more important than a specific reward.

(continued)

demonstrated was that individuals can come to different conclusions about Heinz's actions but share the same level of reasoning skill. For example, Stage 4 thinkers could defend stealing the drug because of one's contractual commitment to a spouse or argue that stealing is wrong because it violates the law.

Research indicates that the average American reasons primarily at Stage 4, the law-and-order orientation. According to Kohlberg, although Stage 4 thinkers will use Stage 5 reasoning occasionally, they will use Stage 3 reasoning as well. He reported that adults can comprehend moral reasoning at one and even two stages higher than their own. They may not be able to produce this higher-stage thinking themselves, but they recognize it and

What's right: I should live up to others' expectations of me.

Why: So people will like me and so I will like myself.

STAGE 4   *Law and order.*

Being good means being a dutiful citizen and obeying the laws set down by those in power.

What's right: I should be a responsible citizen and follow the rules and regulations of society.

Why: To keep the system from falling apart.

STAGE 5   *Social contract.*

The rules of society exist for the benefit of all and are established by mutual agreement. However, if the rules become destructive or if one party doesn't live up to the agreement, the contract is no longer binding.

What's right: I have to be responsive to the needs of others within my society.

Why: To keep my society from falling apart.

STAGE 6   *Universal ethical principles.*

General universal principles determine right and wrong. These values are established by individual reflection and may contradict the egocentric or legal principles of earlier reasoning.

What's right: I have to show the greatest respect for the rights and dignity of all people and support a system that protects human rights.

Why: Because that is what my conscience tells me to do.

Adapted from T. Lickona, 1983, Raising Good Children, New York: Bantam. 1976, *Moral Development and Behavior: Theory Research and Sound Issues,* New York: Holt, Rinehart and Winston.

---

acknowledge it as superior to their own. Kohlberg asserted that this finding was fundamental to moral leadership.

Do we want to encourage the use of higher moral reasoning skills? Is the development of Stages 5 and 6 a goal we should move toward? Generally, Americans want to be people of high principles. In a 1993 Gallup Poll (Elam, Rose, & Gallup), 91 percent of respondents indicated that moral courage was a worthwhile value to be taught.

The respondents also strongly approved (87 percent) the teaching of values in the public schools, specifically honesty, democracy, tolerance, patriotism, caring for friends and family members, moral courage, and the Golden Rule.

In 1992, an eminent and diverse group of educators, youth leaders and ethicists issued the Aspen Declaration, a document that asserted the primacy of six core ethical values that transcend cultural, religious, and socioeconomic differences: trustworthiness, respect, responsibility, fairness and justice, caring, and civic virtue and citizenship. Do you agree that these six values are universal? What do these terms mean to you?

_____

_____

_____

_____

We agree as a nation not only on what values are important, but also that these values should be taught throughout society. Questions arise: Can we teach adults (in this case, real estate practitioners) to be more ethical? Are adult patterns of ethical reasoning too ingrained to accept change? Can we expect practitioners to learn to perform professionally at a higher level than they live their personal lives?

CASE STUDY 3.1   A Real Life Heinz?

Lisa and Larry Archer were married only a short time when they discovered that Lisa had ovarian cancer. Larry spent so much time caring for Lisa as her condition deteriorated that he lost his factory job. He moved his wife and her three children from West Memphis, Tennessee, to Lepanto, Arkansas, a small farming community. They applied for public aid, but the paperwork was lost. Several banks turned down requests for loans. On the morning of November 22, 1994, Archer took his children to school, dropped his wife off at their apartment, and headed to nearby Jonesboro.

At a branch of MidSouth Bank, Mr. Archer passed a note to a teller: "This is a robbery. I want $10,000." Though carrying no weapon, he threatened to blow up the building. The teller gave him all of the money in her cash drawer—$4,150. Archer was captured in less than half an hour. He faces bank robbery charges that could bring 5 to 20 years in prison.

(continued)

CASE STUDY 3.1   Continued.

The Jonesboro police detective handling the case indicated that Mr. Archer later learned that Mrs. Archer had ovarian cysts, not cancer. He also indicated that though the family was financially in dire straits, Mr. Archer refused a number of attempts by the national media to be interviewed, which might have solved his financial problems. Archer pled guilty to the bank robbery.

(Adapted from James Jefferson, "Confessed Bank Robber Says Desperation Drove Him to Commit Crime," *Savannah Morning News,* p. 5C.)

Exercise

If you were the judge, what sentence would you pronounce on Archer?

_____

_____

_____

_____

Ethical Systems

Granma said I had done right, for when you come on something that is good, first thing to do is share it with whoever you can find; that way, the good spreads. . .

Forrest Carter

For hundreds of years, philosophers have expounded on the subject of ethics and how best to conduct a moral life. While there are many noteworthy ethical systems, we will describe four different philosophies here, not only because they are ideas of prominent philosophers but also because they represent differing approaches that real estate practitioners often use.

When asked how to solve a particular dilemma, real estate agents typically respond in one of four ways:

1. I would decide based on what would get the sale of the property and result in a sales commission.
2. I would decide based on what the state or federal statutes or my state licensing board says is legal.
3. I would decide based on what the customs of real estate practice are in my community.
4. I would decide based on what my conscience tells me to do.

These four statements represent four different ethical systems: end-results ethics, rule or law ethics, social contract ethics, and transformational ethics. English philosopher Jeremy Bentham described end-results thinking in the 1700s and argued that an action is ethical if it results in happiness. During the same time, Prussian philosopher Immanuel Kant described an ethical system where individuals stand on principles and restrain themselves by rules and laws. Another 18th-century philosopher, Frenchman Jean–Jacques Rousseau, espoused social contract ethics, wherein the customs and values of the community form the laws and define moral goodness. Martin Buber, a 20th-century philosopher, was one of the foremost proponents of transformational ethics, suggesting that people must rely on their consciences to determine moral action. Each of these philosophers proposed different definitions of and models for ethical behavior, and each system has strengths and limitations.

End-Results Ethics

Real estate agents who consider foremost the consequences of their actions when responding to ethical dilemmas are practicing end-results ethics. These individuals tend to look at problems pragmatically. The end-results practitioner would ask: "How am I to judge what is right or wrong? I can't rely on laws or the practices of other agents. I can only look at the consequences of my own actions."

In the 18th century, English philosopher Jeremy Bentham described this form of thinking as *utilitarianism,* a term based on his assumption that an action has usefulness to the extent that it results in happiness or prevents pain, evil, or unhappiness.

In response to a dilemma, a subscriber to end-results ethics might draw up a chart of pros and cons, see which list is longer, and act accordingly. This individual charts an ethical course based on whether or not a decision makes as many people happy as possible. In other words, an end-results thinker does not see things as "right" or "wrong," but as "desirable" or "undesirable." If an action leads to the greatest possible balance of good consequences or to the least possible balance of bad consequences, an action is ethical.

Some critics suggest that end-results ethics can lead to trouble. End-results thinkers consider happiness and pleasure worthwhile results. But what do happiness and pleasure mean? What causes one person happiness might cause another pain. For example, when considering a ban on smoking in a real estate office, it might seem a good idea, for health reasons, to prohibit smoking in all areas. The majority of employees are nonsmokers, want the ban, and are happy with the decision. The minority smokers, however, feel that not being allowed to smoke would make them irritable and unproductive. They are also concerned about customers and clients who smoke—where can they go if the ban is implemented, or might they just go to a competitor? End-results ethics would be difficult to use in this dilemma because it is difficult to measure happiness and utility here. We cannot justify a decision based on making 80 percent of the office happy and 20 percent unhappy.

End-results ethics also focus on consequence. A benefit of focusing on consequence is the possibility of reducing risk. For example, a client asks an agent not to disclose a physical defect, such as a leaky roof, to prospective buyers. The client has good reason for keeping this information private: buyers who know the roof leaks will want to purchase the property for less. While this may be true, the client may not be considering the possibility of being sued for failure to reveal a latent defect. The cost of a lawsuit could be greater than the cost of repairing the roof.

However, real estate practitioners, particularly novices, cannot always predict the outcome of a particular action. Consider the case study on the following page.

End-results ethics has advantages: it is a common-sense approach that considers everyone who has a stake in the dilemma. But because it fails to define happiness in a consistent manner, end-results ethics cannot be applied universally. It does supply, however, some worthwhile ideas for a model of ethical decision making.

CALVIN AND HOBBES © Watterson. Reprinted with permission of UNIVERSAL PRESS SYNDICATE. All rights reserved.

CASE STUDY 4.1   Don't Be Blind to the Buyers' Source of Money

by Christina Hoffman

If you ever raise an eyebrow about the source of buyers' funds, don't proceed with a transaction before confirming that source. By turning a blind eye to the possibility that a buyer may use illegal funds to purchase a property, you could find yourself in criminal court. That's what happened to a salesperson in Mooresville, North Carolina.

An alleged drug dealer contacted the salesperson to look at houses. Their meetings took place during normal business hours, and the buyer arrived in either a red or gold Porsche. On one occasion, the buyer showed the salesperson a briefcase containing $20,000 in cash to demonstrate that he could buy a house.

The buyer eventually found a house he wanted. After negotiations, the parties agreed on a sales price of $182,500. But the buyer couldn't get a loan for that amount and asked the sellers to accept $60,000 under the table in cash and to lower the sales contract price to $122,500. The sellers agreed, and the buyer secured a loan for $122,500.

The listing salesperson executed a new sales agreement that reflected the lower sales price. She also increased the sales commission. That way, the salesperson would earn as much commission on the new, lower price as on the original price.

The buyer was later arrested on drug charges. The U.S. attorney's office investigated his assets, which included the house. Because the salesperson had helped him buy the property, the U.S. attorney's office indicted her on three counts: money laundering, engaging in a transaction of criminally derived property, and causing a false statement to be filed with government agencies. (The closing documents filed with HUD and the IRS indicated the sales price was $122,500, when it had really been $182,500.)

A district court acquitted her on the money laundering and criminally derived property charges. The government appealed the ruling.

The issue that went before the U.S. Court of Appeals for the Fourth Circuit in the *United States v. Campbell,* 977 F2d 854 (1992), says the salesperson's attorney, James Frank Wyatt III of Charlotte, N.C., was whether the salesperson knew that the buyer's funds came from an illegal source and was, therefore, guilty of money laundering.

The court determined that the buyer's lifestyle (the buyer flashed around large amounts of money, drove expensive cars, and apparently could be away from his business during working hours), the listing salesperson's testimony that the selling salesperson had remarked before closing that the funds may have been "drug money," and the fraudulent transaction that the

(continued)

CASE STUDY 4.1	Continued.

buyer asked the salesperson to participate in should have been enough for a jury to determine that the salesperson was "willfully blind" to the possibility that the buyer was a drug dealer.

The appeals court revised the judgment of acquittal by the lower court and remanded the case for a new trial. At the new trial, the judge dismissed the money-laundering charge but convicted the salesperson of misdemeanor charges on the two other counts. She was sentenced to five years of probation.

How can you avoid such a situation? "Don't accept cash," says Wyatt. "If you're skeptical, ask about the source of funds and suggest that the source be verified, either through bank or business, which would insulate you from liability. If necessary, get the person providing the money to sign an affidavit about the source."

Exercise

In what way could the real estate agent have been using an end-results orientation? What limitations of end-results thinking are demonstrated in this example?

_____

_____

_____

Rule or Law Ethics

The rule thinker is primarily concerned with the importance of rules or laws of a society, believing that effective laws apply to everyone and to all circumstances and are based on fundamental moral truths. One of the most prominent advocates of this ethical system was the 18th-century Prussian philosopher Immanuel Kant. Kant believed that rules and laws should be based on reason, not on usefulness, intuition, or conscience.

Kantian philosophy assumes that laws will be written and enacted by moral people who recognize fundamental principles and truths. Unfortunately, not all human-made rules and ethics are so inspired. One of the disadvantages of following fundamental truths is the difficulty of agreeing upon which truths are fundamental. By what authority do we accept particular truths? How do we know they are good? History is scarred by examples of those who murdered others in the name of their truths. Taken to extreme, rule ethics suggests that a practice is right or wrong based on its legality. Rule thinkers believe they can base decisions on the standards established by the rules. These individuals see little ambiguity in their decisions.

One consequence of following fundamental truths is that the result may be unpleasant. End-results thinkers might not tell clients about all the risks of a particular purchase if it meant losing the sale. A rule thinker would advise of all the risks, if state and federal laws required it, regardless of the consequences.

A concern in using rule ethics is determining which rule to follow when rules conflict. In the real estate business, we often walk an ethical tightrope between the buyer's right to information about a property and a fiduciary obligation to the seller to keep some information confidential. Rule ethics may not help practitioners decide in situations where regulatory commissions and state statutes do not clearly address this type of dilemma.

Another limitation of rule ethics is that for every law or rule—even good ones—there are exceptions to those laws. Consider the case study on the next page.

A rule thinker considering this case would abide by the regulatory commission's policy to publish the names of offenders, mainly because this has been past policy. Neither the broker's restitution nor other circumstances of the case would be relevant to the decision to publish. Those whose orientation is different would weigh the circumstances and perhaps come to another conclusion. Whatever your decision, this ethical dilemma illustrates that exceptions to hard-and-fast rules exist. Rule ethics provide a framework in which to make a decision, just as end-results ethics do, but neither system provides all possible ways of making a decision.

Social Contract Ethics

In contrast to rule thinkers who consider the legalities of an issue first, individuals who consider their community's best interest when making an ethical decision are using social contract ethics. The customs and values of the community serve as the underpinnings of that community's laws. As community members, we submit to those laws, giving up our personal liberty, but receiving civil liberty in exchange. A community can be defined broadly as one's cultural or social group, or more narrowly as one's neighborhood or professional group. The foremost proponent of social contract ethics was the 18th-century French philosopher Jean–Jacques Rousseau.

Real estate practitioners often have an agreement with their employers and colleagues regarding conduct. For example, many brokerage firms use policy and procedures manuals that describe office rules and regulations. The purpose of the manual is to deter conflict and promote harmony. The use of policy manuals is increasingly important for establishing fair and consistent practices in brokerage firms. Furthermore, brokers can use their policy manual to defend against lawsuits that allege unfair or unprofessional conduct by their agents. While agents may not have helped create or shape those policies and procedures, by accepting employment with that broker, they have created a social contract and agreed to abide by that broker's policies. Membership in a local association of REALTORS® also creates a contract whereby members agree to abide by the code of ethics and other bylaws of the organization.

CASE STUDY 4.2 — Exceptions to the Rule?

You are state commissioner on the real estate regulatory board. You have to decide today about an appropriate action on a complaint filed against a broker for mishandling escrow funds.

This appearance is the broker's first before the board. She is 24 years old and has little more than the required years of experience in the business to obtain a broker's license. At the request of her parents, who own a real estate brokerage and who are in failing health, the young woman obtained her broker's license. During the time she was obtaining her license, her parents hired an interim broker who stole $25,000 from the escrow account.

The embezzlement was not discovered until several months after the young woman had taken over the business. Upon discovery, the young broker and her family made complete monetary restitution to all of the clients. Nevertheless, a complaint was filed against the company.

The broker has expressed her regret at not having a proper financial audit performed at the time she took over the company and is completely willing to submit to additional penalties the state might impose. She asks for only one consideration: she is a prominent student at a state university and is a candidate for a scholarship. She requests that her name not be published in the state regulatory newsletter so that she can remain eligible for the scholarship.

It is the regulatory commission's policy to publish the names of offenders in the newsletter to deter inappropriate conduct among licensees. Publishing this case could act as such a deterrent.

Exercise

Should you publish the broker's name and the incident in the newsletter as usual? Why or why not?

Under social contract theory, by becoming a member of a community we agree to be governed by a standard of morality larger than our own. The community's authority is absolute and cannot be challenged or superseded. Individuals opposed to the authority of the community may either abide by the standards or leave. Social contract thinkers believe in helping others and working for the common good.

The problem with social contract ethics is one that has surfaced before: inability to closely define terms. What does the "common good" mean? How do we determine community standards when individuals disagree about those standards? As 19th-century English author Samuel Butler said, "Morality is the custom of one's country and the current feeling of one's peers. Cannibalism is moral in a cannibal country." In the real estate business, there are ongoing discussions about agency representation, facilitation, access to MLS and other databases, and licensing reciprocity, to name a few areas where "community standards" are difficult to determine.

CASE STUDY 4.3   Between a Rock and a Hard Place

A husband and wife asked a real estate broker to assist them in purchasing a property. The couple advised the broker that they had already selected a home after previewing it with a rival firm. Because the broker wanted to avoid any procuring cause battles over the transaction, the broker asked, "Why don't you have the agent who showed you the home write up your offer?"

The wife explained that they had been prepared to let the agent write up the offer but had been offended by an off-color remark the agent made. The broker persisted, "Why don't you ask another agent in the firm or the broker of the firm to assist you instead?" The couple then stated, "It was the broker who made the offensive remark. We refuse to do business with the firm or any of its agents."

What should the broker do? Since few states regulate matters relating to procuring cause, most brokers will have to rely on the standards of their community to resolve this issue. In some communities, it would be appropriate for the second broker to work with the buyers since it was the buyers who solicited the help from the broker. Other practitioners might accuse the second broker of disrupting the natural sequence of business events. Yet others might consider the violation of community standards by using inappropriate language more important and the loss of the buyer's business an appropriate consequence.

While social contract ethics provides the framework for participative democracy and influenced the framers of the U.S. Constitution, this philosophy also has serious weaknesses. Sometimes, the public holds real estate practitioners to higher standards than the practitioners themselves do.

Another limitation is the implication that those who challenge the community will be suppressed or expelled. For example, when buyer brokers attempted to establish themselves, some traditional brokers initially refused to cooperate with them. Some buyer brokers were driven out of business.

Also, social contract theory justifies the supreme authority of the state. If the state or community is not moral—for example, Nazi Germany—should individuals obey it? These are questions that Rousseau and social contract theory leave unanswered. Despite these drawbacks, social contract ethics is another element in building a model of ethical decision making.

Transformational Ethics

In the drama *A Man for All Seasons,* Thomas More responds to his friend and his daughter who are imploring him to betray his principles and thus to save his life, "I will not give in because I oppose it—*I* do—not my pride, not my spleen, nor any other of my appetites but *I* do—*I!* " The hero eloquently expresses that intangible quality known as conscience.

Transformational ethics, unlike end-results, law-and-order, or social contract ethics, seeks to discover the truth that lies within each individual. An individual's personal convictions serve as the ultimate standard when making decisions of ethical dimensions.

Martin Buber, who died in 1965, was one of the foremost proponents of transformational or personal ethics. Buber disagreed with end-results ethics because he believed that unethical actions to serve ethical ends cannot be justified. Buber also adamantly opposed rule ethics, believing that there is rarely time to consult a rule book when confronted with an ethical conflict and that the rules are often wrong anyway. Furthermore, Buber opposed social contract ethics because it suppressed the individual who stood up for his rights.

The term *transformational ethics* suggests that each person brings a unique perspective to an ethical dilemma. Unlike the other philosophies, which focus on the outer world—on consequences, rules, and societal norms—transformational ethics focuses on what lies within each person: conscience. Conscience may be defined as the "voice from within." Some believe the source of conscience to be a higher authority or a divine spark. Martin Luther King Jr., Anwar Sadat, and Mahatma Gandhi all practiced transformational ethics. At great personal sacrifice, they stood up for their personal convictions when confronted with grave ethical problems. Their commitment to conscience transformed them and inspired those around them.

There are limitations to transformational ethics, as there are to the three other ethical systems. Transformational ethics are highly personal. Imagine

Thoughts on Conscience

Whenever you are to do a thing, though it can never be known but to yourself, ask yourself how you would act were all the world looking at you, and act accordingly.

—Thomas Jefferson

Never do anything against conscience even if the state demands it.

—Albert Einstein

Never exchange good conscience for the good will of others to avoid their ill will.

—Charles Simmons

If your conscience won't stop you, pray for cold feet.

—Elmer G. Leterman

If you compromise with your own conscience, you will weaken your conscience. Soon your conscience will fail to guide you and you will never have real wealth based on peace of mind.

—Napoleon Hill

In your secret chamber ere you are judged;
See you do nothing to blush for,
Though but the ceiling looks down upon you.

—Tse-sze, grandson of Confucius

a real estate agent who turned away an unmarried couple who wanted to live together. Consider an agent who declined to find a property for a weapons manufacturing firm. These agents consulted their consciences and refused to represent potential clients.

How would we deal with two agents who have conflicting points of view, both based on a personal ethical code? How could we manage an office if each agent refused to conform to office policy because they made decisions based on their consciences? The limitation of this system is that transformational ethics can become relative ethics: right or wrong is decided by each individual. If practitioners of transformational ethics disregard others' ethical beliefs, they risk becoming outlaws or social outcasts.

Rather than rely on only one test, real estate practitioners should consider them all. Each ethical system[1] has strengths and limitations, sheds light on possible solutions to the problem, and provides part of the answer.

---

[1] For a more thorough discussion of the four ethical systems mentioned in this chapter, the reader may wish to consult William D. Hitt's *Ethics and Leadership*. Columbus, OH: Battelle Press, 1990.

The next challenge is to integrate the advantages of each philosophical orientation into a working model for ethical conduct. Consider which system or systems you would apply to the situation in the case study below.

CASE STUDY 4.4 | Revelations

You are the listing agent of a home in a middle-class neighborhood. Families with young children own many of the properties. People who buy there are looking for a neighborhood with children and a nearby elementary school with a good reputation.

About two years ago, the school board decided to build a new elementary school on power company land. The property was purchased at a reasonable price because of its proximity to a power substation and high-voltage power lines. As the school was constructed, the parents of children who were to attend the school protested the danger of children being exposed to electromagnetic fields (EMFs). The parents cited a number of studies that indicated that chronic exposure to EMFs causes childhood leukemia and other illnesses. The parents' protest was effective in that school officials decided to test EMF levels during the year. No significant results were found, but the school board also decided to give parents the option of sending their children to other schools.

The sellers have asked you not to disclose any information about EMFs. Furthermore, there is no law in your state indicating that real estate agents must reveal the possible presence of EMFs. Reports that you have read on EMFs are contradictory and confusing. You know, however, that houses near high-tension power lines have devalued in price. If you disclose to prospective purchasers that children who live in this neighborhood may attend a school with a potential environmental hazard, you may limit the number of good offers that the sellers receive.

Exercise

How would you handle this dilemma?

_____

_____

_____

EXERCISE

Consider which of the following tests you applied in deciding how to handle the dilemma in Case Study 4.4. How would:

1. Those who have an end-results orientation *test for results?*

_____

_____

_____

_____

2. Those who have a rule orientation *test for laws and policies?*

_____

_____

_____

_____

3. Those who have a social contract orientation *test for community values?*

_____

_____

_____

_____

4. Those who have a transformational or personal orientation *test for conscience?*

_____

_____

_____

_____

Models for Ethical Decision-Making

'Tis the business of little minds to shrink; but he whose heart is firm, and whose conscience approves his conduct, will pursue his principles unto death.

Thomas Paine

In *Ethics: Theory and Practice,* Jacques Thiroux suggests that for an ethical system to work effectively, it should be:

1. Rational but not without emotion;
2. Logical but not rigid or inflexible;
3. General enough to apply universally yet apply to specific individuals and situations; and
4. Able to resolve conflicts among societal needs and individual needs

End-results ethics, rule ethics, social contract ethics, or transformational ethics alone cannot meet Thiroux's criteria. Used together, however, these four philosophies compose a rational model for ethical decision making. Consider the dilemma described in the case study on the next page.

CASE STUDY 5.1   The Case of the Murder–Suicide

A real estate salesperson is called to meet an owner of a home in a middle-class suburb. The property looks somewhat run down: the lawn has not been tended, litter is strewn about, the inside is vacant.

The owner of the home shows the property to the agent. When the agent asks why he wants to sell, the owner looks embarrassed and says, "Look, this property belonged to my cousin. About six months ago, he murdered his family here and then committed suicide. I inherited this property through the probate court's decision, and I want to get rid of it as quickly as possible. Tell me what to ask for, so I can be done with this mess."

While other similar properties in the area have been selling for about $120,000, the agent knows that when buyers find out that the property was the scene of a murder–suicide, the seller will be lucky to get $100,000.

Exercise

What should the agent do when buyers ask why the seller is offering the property? Should the agent disclose this information?

_____

_____

_____

_____

Let's consider the model on the facing page for coping with this ethical dilemma. This model of ethical decision making is based on the assumption that *no single ethical philosophy can provide a complete solution to an ethical dilemma.* On the other hand, integrating the best of all the philosophies and considering the dilemma from all perspectives is more likely to result in the "most correct" response. For example, in the murder–suicide dilemma, we must first consider what we know about the problem. The *facts* about the dilemma include the following:

- The seller is motivated to sell the property.
- The property appears distressed.
- Comparable property value is approximately $120,000.

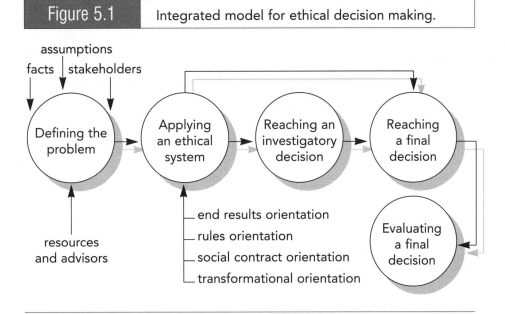

Figure 5.1 — Integrated model for ethical decision making.

Our *assumptions* about the dilemma are:

- The property will sell beneath market value because of its condition and the seller's motivation.
- The neighbors are aware of the murder–suicide on the property, but others might not know of the tragedy, particularly out-of-town prospects. A neighbor, however, is likely to tell any prospective buyer about the tragedy, either before or after the closing.
- The seller told the agent about the murder–suicide in confidence.
- Some buyers might want to know about the murder–suicide, either because they are superstitious or because they could get better terms or a better price on a stigmatized property.

We know that a number of people are *stakeholders* in the agent's decision to disclose or not disclose the information:

- *The agent.* A listing and possible commission may be at risk; the agent may be sued by the seller for revealing the information to the buyer; the buyer may sue if this information is withheld.
- *The seller.* The best price and terms may be at risk if the agent reveals that the property has been the scene of a murder–suicide; however, if the agent withholds this information, the seller may be sued later.
- *Prospective buyers.* Buyers may pay too much if they are not fully aware of the stigmas attached to the property; buyers may regret purchasing the property if they find out about the stigma after the fact and may have to sue responsible parties.

- *Superiors.* The broker–manager may wish to reject the listing or accept the listing with or without reservations regarding disclosure.

- *Peers.* Colleagues may find this listing undesirable and may not want to show it.

- *Subordinates.* Office staff may regard this listing as undesirable and may not feel comfortable answering questions from co-brokers and prospective buyers.

- *Family.* Family members may regard this property as unsavory and may be unsupportive.

- *Community.* Neighbors may be worried about how the sale of this property will affect their own market values; they may be willing to reveal the murder–suicide to all prospective buyers.

In defining the problem, we should also consider potential *resources and advisors.* In the Case of the Murder–Suicide, other real estate practitioners who have experienced similar problems may be an excellent source of advice. Real estate magazines and periodicals may also offer guidance. Professionals such as attorneys, clergy, psychologists, and teachers can provide different perspectives on the problem as well. Certainly, the office broker should be consulted.

As the Integrated Model for Ethical Decision Making illustrates, the facts, assumptions, and stakeholders define the problem. In addition to considering the feelings and possible concerns of any and all stakeholders, the agent may also consider using different ethical systems. How would a real estate practitioner who practices end-results ethics consider the dilemma? What about a rule-oriented practitioner? A social contract thinker? A transformational thinker?

1. *End-results orientation:*
   - What will the consequences of my action be if I take the listing and keep the murder–suicide confidential?
   - What will the consequences of my action be if I take the listing and disclose information about the murder–suicide to prospective buyers?

2. *Rule orientation:*
   - What are the state laws, rules, and regulations regarding disclosure of such matters?

3. *Social contract orientation:*
   - What does the policy and procedures manual of my office require? What does my professional code of conduct advise? What would my brokers and peers expect? What does society (friends, family, and neighbors) expect?

4. *Transformational orientation:*

  ■ What does my conscience tell me to do?

Consider possible answers to these concerns:

  ■ *What will the consequences of my action be if I take the listing and keep the murder–suicide confidential?*
  I will keep the seller happy for the short term, but the long-term risk is great. The buyers may sue the seller for withholding material information. As an agent, I could also be held responsible.

  ■ *What will the consequences of my action be if I take the listing and disclose information about the murder–suicide to all prospective buyers?*
  The buyers may appreciate knowing this information but may also be reluctant to make an offer. Buyers may make low offers. Disclosure may harm the seller, and if done without the seller's permission, may be considered a breach of fiduciary relationship.

  ■ *What are the state laws, rules, and regulations regarding disclosure of such matters?*
  Some state's laws, such as California's, require that a crime such as a murder–suicide be disclosed if committed within three years of marketing the home. My state does not yet have a law or court case that will aid my decision.

  ■ *What does the policy and procedures manual of my office require?*
  My policy and procedures manual reminds me to keep the seller's interests above those of others.

  ■ *What does my professional code of conduct advise?*
  My professional code of ethics advises me to keep the seller's interests above those of others, but also reminds me to be honest with the buyers.

  ■ *What would my brokers and peers expect?*
  The broker/owners of my firm would want me to take the listing but would want to know all the circumstances so they could decide how to market it appropriately. My peers might feel uncomfortable with the listing.

  ■ *What does society (friends, family, and neighbors) expect?*
  My major concern is the neighbors. They want the property sold because it is poorly maintained. They also are worried that the home has a "reputation" that could damage property values in the area.

  ■ *What does my conscience tell me to do?*
  I think buyers have a right to know, not only the material and physical defects of the property, but anything within reason that might adversely affect the future value of the home. I would like to be able to give this information to prospective buyers. On the other hand, I respect my seller's right to a fiduciary relationship.

By speculating about possible decisions and their outcomes, the agent is practicing investigatory decision making; that is, experimenting with hypothetical results of a particular decision, a process that can help the agent reach a final decision.

What might the final decision be? If the agent integrates the responses to all of the questions, the following scenario is likely:

> I will inform the seller that I would like the listing on this property. I will explain the seller's right to keep certain information, such as the tragedy that took place on this property, confidential. I will also explain, however, that a seller's right to confidentiality sometimes conflicts with the buyer's right to know, as in this case.
>
> While the courts and the legislature in this state have not yet spoken on the issue of disclosure about murder or other crimes on marketed property, I would certainly not want my seller to be the test case, nor would I want an angry buyer to name my brokerage firm in a lawsuit. While I may not disclose this information to the buyer, a neighbor is likely to.
>
> I will ask the seller to give me the listing and allow me to reveal the information to prospective buyers at an appropriate point. I would like this permission in writing. I will discuss these issues with my broker, and if the listing is acceptable on these terms, we will have a special marketing session with the other agents in the firm to discuss how to handle questions about the murder–suicide. We will do our best to get the seller the highest price possible under the circumstances—for the seller's sake as well as for the neighborhood's sake.

While other responses to this ethical dilemma are possible, use the following questions to evaluate the above solution.

- Have you defined the problem accurately?
- How would you define the problem if you were the buyer? The seller? Your broker? Your peers? The neighbors?
- To whom did you give your loyalty first and foremost? Was that the appropriate choice?
- Could your decision harm anyone?
- Did (or can or should) you discuss this decision with anyone else?
- Would your response to this dilemma be the same tomorrow? One year from now? Ten years from now?

Apply the Integrated Model for Ethical Decision Making (refer back to Figure 5.1) to the case study on the next page.

| CASE STUDY 5.2 | Murder–Suicide Haunts Owners |

When home buyer Corinne Roslund noticed little spots on the wood-work and the wall and attempted to clean them, the spots came off red on her sponge. Later, a neighborhood boy rode by on a bicycle and called the home "the murder house." Roslund became suspicious, called the local police, and discovered that in 1987, a murder–suicide had taken place on the property. A 38-year-old mother, apparently upset over an impending divorce, shot her 8-year-old daughter and 10-year-old son, and then shot herself. Only the boy survived.

No one, including the real estate agent and the dead woman's husband, told Roslund or her husband about the crime. Neighbors in the affluent Boca Raton, Florida, neighborhood knew about the tragedy, but did not inform the Roslunds. Mr. and Mrs. Roslund began having nightmares about death and couldn't stop thinking about the shooting. Two years after they purchased the home, the Roslunds decided to sell and move away. A month after putting the home on the market, they sued the listing firm, its agent, the mortgage company, and the former owner for failing to disclose the property's history. They also abandoned the house and stopped making mortgage payments. A foreclosure cost them their credit rating and $80,000 in lost equity.

Ironically, the Roslund's present real estate agent felt obligated to tell potential buyers about the history of the property. She claimed that revealing this information lost the Roslunds several interested buyers.

The case was settled out of court.

The Kew Gardens Principle

Real estate agents may face ethical dilemmas where "doing no harm" is not the appropriate response. Avoiding doing harm may be the best response to the conflict between a buyer's right to know about a murder–suicide on a property and the seller's right to confidentiality. But what are the ethical implications of avoiding injury to one party if the full range of possible moral actions has not been exhausted? Consider the case study below.

You may find that your best response to the "Case of the Child Molester" leaves you less than satisfied in this instance. For example, you may have legal concerns about the buyer's right to live anywhere he wishes that directly conflict with your personal suspicions about his rehabilitation because he is choosing to live near an elementary school. Your desire to do what is right for the seller also conflicts with the potential harm to the community if the buyer completes this transaction and then commits another sex offense. Your response may depend upon whether or not the legal system can do any more than it already has by incarceration. While you know that legally you must present the offer, you might debate whether you should submit it, knowing that the owners might accept.

CASE STUDY 5.3 | The Case of the Child Molester

An agent takes a listing on a residential property adjacent to an elementary school. A chain-link fence marks the boundary between the backyard and school property. The owners are motivated to sell and price the property reasonably. The agent puts a yard sign on the front lawn, and in a few days, an interested buyer asks to see the home. During the showing, the buyer says that he is willing to make a full-price offer on the property. It is somewhat unusual in this marketplace for buyers to submit full-price offers, but the agent is delighted to do so, confident that a commission is on the horizon.

After writing up the offer and having the buyer sign it, the agent makes an appointment with the sellers to present the offer. Before leaving for his appointment, however, the agent reads the afternoon paper. On the front page is a picture of the potential buyer with a story about his recent release from prison for serving his sentence for child molestation, abduction, and a host of other offenses related to children.

Exercise

How does the real estate agent's dilemma in this case differ from the dilemma in the murder–suicide case? What are some of the ethical concerns that the agent now faces? What should the agent do if the sellers decide to sell to this buyer with full knowledge of his criminal past? How would this dilemma be resolved differently if the agent worked for the buyer? Use the model developed in this chapter to respond to this dilemma.

_____

_____

_____

_____

Once the sellers accept the offer, you may wonder if you should take a course of action to obstruct the contract, such as picketing the property. To do so might be a breach of fiduciary to the seller and could even leave you open to a lawsuit by the buyer. However, the buyer's criminal record may have negatively affected his credit so that a loan contingency clause in the contract cannot be met. Thus the sales contract itself could resolve this dilemma.

In the murder–suicide dilemma, it may have been sufficient to do no harm. In that case, you had a responsibility to see that your actions did not harm the seller, the buyer, or any other parties. In the molestation case, it may be a higher priority to help others.

Under these circumstances, it is helpful to consider a model of ethical decision making called the Kew Gardens Principle, which is based on the four factors outlined in the box below. The Kew Gardens Principle is named for a shocking New York City homicide case in the 1960s. A young woman, Kitty Genovese, was brutally attacked and murdered in front of 30 or more apartment dwellers, safe inside their homes, none of whom called police or even screamed. Note that any one of the four factors associated with the principle may compel an individual to act. However, the principle suggests that we have a greater moral obligation to act when these factors occur simultaneously.

Kew Gardens Principle

An agent has an increased moral obligation to aid another person based on four factors:

Need There is a clear need for aid (for example, harm has been or is about to be done).

Proximity The agent is "close" to the situation (not necessarily in space, but in terms of notice), knows of the need, or could reasonably be held responsible for knowing.

Capability The agent has means to aid the person in need without taking undue risk.

Last Resort No one else is likely to help. The first three factors create a presumption to aid the person in need. This presumption is strengthened to the degree that the agent is the only one who can render help. Given our propensity to fail to act on the false assumption that others will do so, it is important to assess this consideration carefully and to give the other three factors greater weight.

From D. G. Jones, 1982. *Doing Ethics in Business.* © 1982 by Oelgeschlager, Gunn, and Hain, Cambridge, MA. Reprinted by permission.

Review the case of the child molester again, but this time consider the four elements of the Kew Gardens Principle:

Is there a clear *need* for aid?

_____

_____

How *close* is the agent to the situation?

_____

_____

How *capable* is the agent?

_____

_____

Is anyone else likely to help? *(last resort)*

_____

_____

After reviewing these four elements, is your response to the molestation dilemma the same or different? Why or why not? Which model of ethical decision making, the *Integrated Model* or the *Kew Gardens Principle,* helped you resolve this dilemma more appropriately?

A practitioner's decision to disclose the buyer's past may be influenced by a law signed into effect in 1996 by President Clinton. "Megan's Law," named after seven-year-old Megan Kanka who was murdered by a neighbor with a history of sex offenses, requires that local officials be warned when dangerous child molesters and rapists are freed from jail and move into their communities. While the law outlines the responsibilities of law enforcement officials, its impact on real estate licensees is uncertain. Although Megan's Law does not require practitioners to disclose the whereabouts of sex offenders, it also does not relieve real estate licensees of ethical obligations to the community.

The murder–suicide and child molester dilemmas raise issues that we hope real estate practitioners will not encounter. However, less serious but still troubling dilemmas face real estate agents in work with colleagues, employers, competitors, and the public. Can other models of ethical decision making help?

A Rational Model of Ethical Analysis

As no single ethical system can provide all the answers to moral dilemmas, no single decision-making model can provide the right structure for everyone's way of thinking about such issues. Analyze the scenario in this case study, a typical problem encountered in a real estate brokerage.

Obviously, the type of ethical problem discussed in the box below differs from the case of the murder–suicide and the case of the child molester. First, the potential harm is limited. While the broker's decision can hurt one of the employees, the injury will remain fairly local—unlike the murder–suicide or child molester cases. Second, the issue of client/customer seniority could have been anticipated.

CASE STUDY 5.4 | A Case of Seniority

When Mark was serving on floor duty last Tuesday, a customer, George Hopkins, called in requesting information about a storefront property listed for rent with the firm. Mark gave the appropriate information to the customer, wrote down Mr. Hopkins' name and phone number, and promised to get back to him within a few days with some other storefront rental possibilities.

Two days later, Mr. Hopkins called back but could not remember Mark's name. Jennifer was on floor duty that morning and tried to find out who had assisted him earlier in the week. She was unsuccessful because there was no telephone log book nor an office policy on the matter. After checking with the office manager, she made an appointment with Mr. Hopkins to show him several properties and successfully negotiated a lucrative long-term lease.

When Mark called Mr. Hopkins back, the customer informed him that one of Mark's colleagues already helped him conclude his search. The property that Mr. Hopkins had agreed to rent was one that Mark had intended to show him. Mark was very angry that Jennifer had "stolen his customer" and threatened to quit the firm if he did not receive the commission on this transaction. Mark is a top producer and has worked for the firm for over five years. Jennifer, on the other hand, is relatively new to the business and to the firm. As a matter of fact, this transaction is only her second.

EXERCISE

As the broker of this firm, what do you consider the ethical dimensions of this issue?

The model of decision making below, proposed by Donald Jones of Drew University, not only offers a procedure to resolve ethical problems, but also recommends forming policies to help prevent their recurrence.

A Rational Model of Ethical Analysis and Decision Making

ANTICIPATORY ETHICS

Step One   State the ethical dilemma in plain language.

Step Two   Identify relevant facts, ranking them in order of significance.

Step Three Identify relevant values/principles.

Step Four   List alternative courses of action.

Step Five   Rank values in preferential scale. Rank predictable consequences in terms of certain harmful or beneficial effects. Make your decision.

Step Six   Adopt a proactive posture and propose a policy or institutional arrangement for preventing this kind of ethical dilemma from recurring.

From D. G. Jones, 1982. *Doing Ethics in Business.* © 1982 by Oelgeschlager, Gunn, and Hain, Cambridge, MA. Reprinted by permission.

Now let's apply the Jones model of decision making to "A Case of Seniority."

STEP ONE   *State the ethical dilemma in plain language.*

Mark, a valuable member of the firm, wants compensation on the Hopkins lease contract based on the fact that Mr. Hopkins called him first. Jennifer, following her manager's request to help the customer, was the procuring cause of the sale. Who is entitled to compensation?

STEP TWO   *Identify relevant facts, ranking them in order of significance.*

1. Jennifer secured the contract.

2. Jennifer followed the recommendation of her manager in working with this client.

3. Mark did make an effort to work with Mr. Hopkins. It is not his fault that the customer called back before Mark could assist him. However, Mark should have made a better effort to ensure that the customer asked for him.

4. Mark is a top producer; Jennifer's potential as a salesperson is uncertain. The wrong move here could discourage her and send a negative signal to the rest of the sales force.

STEP THREE   *Identify relevant values.*

1. Maintaining harmony and cooperation between office colleagues.
2. Providing agents with a sense of broker support.
3. Being fair.

STEP FOUR   *List alternative courses of action.*

1. Give the entire commission to Mark.
2. Give the entire commission to Jennifer.
3. Split the commission between Mark and Jennifer equally.
4. Give Mark a percentage equal to a referral fee from Jennifer's portion of the commission.
5. Give Mark a percentage equal to a referral fee from the office portion of the commission.

STEP FIVE   *Rank values in preferential scale. Rank predictable consequences in terms of certain harmful or beneficial effects. Make your decision.*

1. Maintaining harmony and cooperation between office colleagues.

    Giving either Mark or Jennifer the entire commission could send a signal to them and the other sales people that getting credit for a sale is more important than the sale itself, that failing to give the customer your name is an acceptable practice, and that a commission is more important than your coworkers.

2. Providing agents with a sense of broker support.

    Giving one party or the other the entire commission makes the office look like the broker is playing favorites based on productivity, seniority, or even gender.

3. Being fair.

    Taking part of a commission from someone following the verbal instructions of the manager undermines the manager's leadership and gives the impression that someone who does not follow good business practices will get compensated anyway.

STEP SIX   *Adopt a proactive posture and propose a policy or institutional arrangement for preventing this kind of ethical dilemma from recurring.*

Because the office was partially at fault for not having a telephone log, the broker agrees to pay Mark a referral fee from the office side of the commission. Because Jennifer followed verbal office policy, she should not be asked to share her commission.

The office will immediately make a telephone log available. Customers and clients who are not properly logged in will be given to the person on floor duty. A policy manual will be written with a specific directive regarding customer and client seniority.

Rotarian Model for Ethical Decision-Making

Members of Rotary International encourage high ethical standards in business and professions. Rotarians commit themselves to a four-step course of action in their personal and business lives. When an ethical dilemma arises, Rotarians ask themselves four questions:

- Is it the truth?
- Will it build good will and better friendships?
- Is it fair to all concerned?
- Is it beneficial to all concerned?

No matter which model we use to help resolve an ethical dilemma, our final course of action is open to public and professional scrutiny. How will our peers judge us? How will the public view our response?

"Before I answer your question about the ethics of the matter, first tell me . . . how much commission is involved?"

Professional Perspectives

The law is not an end in itself, nor does it provide ends. It is preeminently a means to serve what we think is right.

Justice William J. Brennan, Jr.

In previous chapters, we reviewed models for ethical decision making and discussed community or public standards of conduct, standards that are particularly important to those practitioners who prize social contract ethics. As real estate agents, we are under the public's constant scrutiny for a number of reasons:

1. *We are a highly visible group.* In 1998, the Association of Real Estate License Law Officials (ARELLO) reported over 1,000,000 licensed brokers and salespeople in the U.S. and Canada.

2. *Our work has a high profile.* We are in the public eye as we help others buy, sell, and lease real estate.

3. *We have the largest trade association in the U.S.* The National Association of REALTORS®, which represents over 700,000 real estate practitioners, occupies a respected presence in Washington, where it lobbies for property rights and related issues.

4. *The subject of real estate is a fascinating one.* The public never tires discussing or reading about it, and many books and newspaper columns are written every day on the subject. Furthermore, because real estate investments can involve large sums of money, these transactions attract media attention, not all of it positive.

When real estate practitioners take advantage of others, public suspicions that they are unscrupulous and unethical are confirmed. Consider the headline story described in the case study below.

CASE STUDY 6.1	Broker Defrauded Widow, 74, in House Sale, Lawsuit Alleges

W hen Ozona Hagans sold her Fort Lauderdale home in March, the new owner ended up paying $50,000.

But, even though Hagans owed less than $10,000 on the mortgage, the 74-year-old widow received only a little more than $9,000 for her home in the 100 block of Northwest Third Avenue.

That is because Hagans's real estate broker, Jack A. Dillon, first sold the house for $39,000 to his own company, American Capital Investment Corp., according to a lawsuit filed by Lula Mae Scott, Hagans's niece.

Dillon then charged about $30,000 in fees and expenses, including a 12 percent sales commission, to the ailing, hard-of-hearing woman, said Scott's attorney, Richard Beauchamp. "The killer is this: The same day as the closing, they turned around and sold [the house] to a third party for $50,000."

Adapted from the *Fort Lauderdale News,* 6 February 1990.

Popular images of real estate agents in such films as *Wall Street, The Money Pit,* and *Lethal Weapon*—though they were minor characters—are also unflattering. These characters are loud mouthed, flashy, and utterly lacking in professionalism. These stereotypes do not accurately represent the majority of honest, hard-working real estate agents.

Nevertheless, these stereotypes and the minority of unethical practitioners who reinforce such negative images pose a major barrier to public recognition of the real estate industry as a *profession;* it is instead most often characterized as a trade or business. Actually, any group that can distinguish itself by virtue of a distinct task or tools may call itself a profession. However, the true characteristics of a profession are the ethical considerations of the group, rather than its techniques or tools. While many disagree about the meaning of the term *profession,* most agree on the following characteristics:

- A clearly defined field of expertise that distinguishes it from others
- A period of education or training prior to membership

- A procedure for testing, licensing, and relicensing generally approved by a state agency under guidance from the profession itself
- A dedication to meeting obligations to society and an emphasis on service over income and wealth as a primary motivator
- A provision for free services to those who cannot afford them
- The application of a sliding scale of fees according to circumstances or ability to pay
- A set of self-governing rules that instill a code of ethics regarding relationship among members and toward society
- A means of self-governance, including the application of penalties for inappropriate behavior or negligence

It would be difficult to argue that *any* group—doctors, attorneys, plumbers, educators, let alone real estate practitioners—can meet all these criteria. Nevertheless, we can argue that real estate practitioners provide special services at a high level of skill and expertise as well as meet many other guidelines that define a profession. What is arguable is whether we can self-govern our ethical conduct.

Because real estate practitioners have expertise, we are permitted to a certain extent to establish the scope and limitations of our role. Because the public does not know precisely what it needs from us, we have been able to devise our own code of ethics. Unfortunately, we have been unable to govern ourselves effectively in this manner, so state legislatures have had to create regulatory licensing laws.

Partly to gain recognition as a profession, members of NAR developed a code of conduct in 1913. Today's *Code of Ethics* contains 17 articles that outline members' responsibilities to clients, customers, fellow REALTORS®, and others.

Professional Practice Standards

The *Code of Ethics: National Association of Realtors®* is an example of professional practice standards, one of two tests used to examine reasonableness in business conduct. (The other test, discussed later in this chapter, is the reasonable person standard.) In civil court cases, the Code is often cited as the norm for conduct in the real estate business. Beauchamp and Bowie (1988), authors of *Ethical Theory and Business,* cite these necessary elements of a professional practice standard:

- Customary practices of a professional community determine duties and other standards of moral conduct.

- A business person is charged professionally with various responsibilities (for example, avoiding harm, honoring warranties, removing conflicts of information, and obeying legal requirements) and must use proper professional criteria to determine appropriate actions.

- Custom in the profession establishes the standards of obligatory conduct, such as due care.

- Because those without expert knowledge are unqualified to establish standards, the professional community is the best source of standards. (pp. 22–23)

While the professional practice standard is a popular one in business, the *Code of Ethics: National Association of Realtors®* illustrates the shortcomings of such standards. For example, the Code is in constant flux due to changing laws and practices around the country. The dynamic nature of the Code shows continuing debate over the role and application of professional codes of conduct. One problem is that the complex issues in the real estate profession cannot be reduced entirely to a simple statement or broad code. Another concern is over the potential gap between the ethical requirements of a society and the current standards of any one group. For example, the issue of agency representation has been around for decades, but not until consumer and media groups began exploring buyer brokerage and facilitation did most professionals deal seriously with this issue. This time lag demonstrates that, under some circumstances, it is not the professional who possesses the most relevant standard. Sometimes, customers and clients demand a higher standard than practitioners themselves.

While the Code is not always completely current in terms of community standards, it is an important guide for local associations of REALTORS® who are responsible for dealing with misconduct, such as invoking disciplinary measures and suspending membership privileges. Unfortunately, only members of the association are subject to disciplinary measures. Nonmembers are not subject to ethical reviews by peers. In addition, the Code does not address specific circumstances. These types of cases often find their way to civil court, where the Code is used as evidence to establish the standard of care or where the community imposes its own standards of conduct.

Reasonable Person Standard

In some cases, we may choose to use another test of reasonableness in business conduct referred to as the *reasonable person standard*. Beauchamp and Bowie (1988) describe the elements of this standard as follows:

- Customers or public representatives judge whether professional determinations are adequate according to standards of reasonableness.

- A professional's conduct may be found negligent or otherwise deficient even if the conduct conforms perfectly to recognized and routine professional practice.

- The reasonable person standard is objective in that it is designed to incorporate the common body of assumptions that members of a society make about their fellow citizens in order to coexist. (The reasonable person is an abstract composite of reasonable persons in society and should never be understood as a specific person or as the average person.) (pp. 23–24)

In many cases, the professional practice standard and the reasonable person standard will result in the same conclusion: the real estate practitioner was (or was not) negligent. In other circumstances, the reasonable person standard is tougher: it considers what the average practitioner needs to know about risks, alternatives, and consequences to make an informed decision and does not consider routine practices in the real estate business.

Consider the case study on the next page. In many situations, ethical dilemmas are resolved privately, where no one is aware of our thoughts or actions and where we are not held up to the scrutiny of our peers and colleagues. We may ask, "Who will know? Who will catch me?" Indeed, Mr. Brooks may have reasoned in this way. In this tragic case, Vermont law sharply rebuked Brooks's moral failure. But what if state statutes do not address disclosure policy? What is the role of the licensee's personal code of ethics in relationship to the law? What if our personal code conflicts with legal requirements?

Ethics and the Law

In an earlier chapter, we discussed the relationship between the laws of state and community (social contract ethics) and the laws of conscience (transformational ethics). In most instances, real estate agents can satisfy their conscience and satisfy state statutes and regulations and professional standards. Sometimes, though, what is legal is not ethical, and what is ethical is not legal. In other instances, state statutes do not address a specific ethical dilemma, leaving the real estate practitioner without guidance.

Let's examine such a conflict: Imagine that you are showing homes in various neighborhoods to an African–American couple. While they are viewing a particular property, a next-door neighbor confronts you outside and threatens the prospects if they buy that property. He insinuates that other neighbors feel the same way he does.

What should you do? The Civil Rights Acts of 1866 and 1968 tell us that buyers cannot be discriminated against because of race. Clearly, if you steer this couple away from the property because of their race, you will vio-

CASE STUDY 6.2	Failure to Disclose Causes Three Deaths

The state of Vermont charged REALTOR®/seller Stephen C. Brooks with involuntary manslaughter in the deaths of three members of a family that purchased his home.

According to court records, Brooks had been warned at least twice that the gas-fired boiler in his basement had a lethal defect. Prosecutors maintain that Brooks never informed John and Linda Cifarelli that the boiler leaked carbon monoxide. A year before Brooks sold his home, his own wife and daughter had been overcome by fumes and had to be hospitalized. Documents show that three days later, a plumbing company repairman found a wire mesh screen blocking the exhaust vent, forcing fumes to back up into the house. The screen was covering the vent to keep out insects and blowing debris. The repairman warned Brooks to leave the boiler off and then notified Vermont Gas Systems of the faulty boiler. Vermont Gas repairmen advised Brooks it was unsafe to operate the boiler and rendered the unit inoperable.

The Cifarelli family purchased the home in September 1988. Three months later, John Cifarelli started the boiler, which was used in a driveway de-icing system, for the first time. While his family slept, carbon monoxide from the boiler filled the home. A houseguest, awakened by a noise in the middle of the night, opened a window and survived. The Cifarellis' five-month-old daughter also survived. Killed, however, were Cifarelli, 34, his pregnant wife Linda, 26, and daughter Nina, 2.

According to prosecutor William Sorrell, it is the first time the state's real estate disclosure law has been used in a manslaughter case. "To my knowledge, the involuntary manslaughter statute has not been used for a death resulting from a hidden defect in a piece of real property," Sorrell told the *Boston Globe.*

According to newspaper accounts, Brooks received a four-year sentence. The court found that failure to disclose the information constituted voluntary manslaughter. It is expected that Brooks will also face additional civil action. Though Brooks is a licensee and a REALTOR®, he was not acting as a broker in this sale, but only as a seller.

Exercise	

To which standard would you hold Brooks? How would the professional practice standard hold him accountable? The reasonable person standard?

late the law. (If you are working for the seller, you may also be breaching fiduciary—another legal obligation—if you suggest that this property is not suitable on racial grounds.) On the other hand, if you do not warn them and they are later harmed, you would feel personally responsible. Your conscience tells you to advise the buyers about the threat and let them draw their own conclusions.

Let's look at another conflict between statutes and conscience: Your non-licensed best friend is in financial difficulty. She is unemployed and unable to pay her mortgage. She sends a relative to you who is looking for a long-term commercial lease. Within a few weeks, you successfully negotiate a transaction and receive a five-figure commission. You would like to express your gratitude for this lucrative referral to your financially strapped friend with a generous cash fee.

What should you do? Your conscience tells you to share the commission with your friend. However, state laws advise that sharing a commission, in any way, with an unlicensed person is a violation, one that could earn you an administrative penalty, including a suspension or loss of license.

These conflicts between the law and ethics pose enormous personal challenges for most of us. Some real estate practitioners would risk following their conscience; they would warn the couple of the potential danger of buying the home or would share the commission with a friend—and suffer the consequences. Others might follow the letter of the law and obey federal and state statutes regardless of individual circumstances.

While either approach can be justified, it is sometimes possible to resolve ethical problems without compromising either the law or your conscience. Often other solutions are available—if only we can see them. In the case of the racist neighbor, the following options exist:

- Advise the neighbor of the Civil Rights Acts and the potential consequences of his own behavior (the seller, the broker, and all potential buyers could sue).

- Hate laws or local ordinances may be in effect for this community, in which case you could report the racist neighbor and allow the legal system to deal with the problem.

- Introduce the neighbor to the prospective buyers and allow them to decide for themselves what kind of neighbors they would be.

- Inform the sellers that the neighbor is making it difficult to market the property and ask them to deal with the problem.

- Inform *all* prospects about the neighbor's threats and let them decide if they are still interested in the property.

- Contact civil rights organizations for help and advice.

EXERCISE

In the case of the unlicensed friend who needs financial help, what legal and ethical options could you consider?

_____

_____

_____

_____

_____

_____

Should these options seem unworkable, you may have to consider other alternatives. Consider that laws attempt to express the least acceptable form of behavior that society will accept but do not inspire us to be our best. The law states, "Thou shalt not murder." The law does not say, "Be good to your neighbor." It is your conscience that encourages you to reach higher than the law.

Nevertheless, following your conscience instead of the law can impose severe risk. Remember Henry David Thoreau and Civil Disobedience? Recall Joan of Arc? Galileo? While following your conscience in real estate transactions rarely results in jail or death, the consequences can be severe nevertheless. Conversely, the loss of your personal integrity, should you compromise your conscience, can also be painful.

One of life's less satisfying lessons is learning to tolerate ambiguity. Few situations are totally bad or good, black or white, which is why few "right" answers to complex moral issues exist. We must try to create several good solutions to a dilemma, make the best decision possible under the circumstances, and then act upon it.

Applying Ethics:
Agency

Most states require agency disclosure. But the requirements of how and when the disclosure is made vary from state to state.

Of all the controversial issues that try the souls of real estate practitioners, none rankles more than that of agency. Even state regulators have not been able to create rules or regulations that fully and satisfactorily deal with the complex issue of agency relationships. Very broadly, an agent is someone who represents the interests of one person in dealing with another. An agent offers expertise and a fiduciary relationship that usually includes legal and ethical responsibilities, such as loyalty, confidentiality, full disclosure of all known facts, obedience, reasonable skill and care, and accountability.

Many professionals can act as agents: physicians, attorneys, and accountants as well as real estate practitioners. But few professionals work so closely with two parties with such divergent interests as do real estate agents. Agents who work *for* sellers frequently work *with* buyers, and, almost as often, agents who work *for* buyers also work *with* sellers—in the same transaction. The majority of states and the District of Columbia require that regardless of whom the agent represents—whether buyer, seller, neither, or both—the parties who are unrepresented must be made aware of this agency relationship. Some states require only that agency relationships be disclosed before the signing of a contractual offer. The majority of states requires that the disclosure be made very early in the relationship between the practitioner and the parties to the transaction and confirmed again at the time of the contract.

In addition to dealing with these various disclosure requirements, agents must also grapple with the naturally complex relationship that exists between buyers and sellers. In the past, the practitioner who worked with the buyer was, in actuality, a subagent of the seller, an individual the subagent probably had never met. Although this cooperating subagent typically developed a friendly, trusting relationship with the buyers, she did not work for them. Ironically, in many such transactions, the buyers treated the practitioner as *their* agent while the seller treated her as a member of the enemy camp. It's no wonder that agents became confused about their loyalties!

Part of the confusion surrounding the agency relationship was that our conscience told us we work for the people with whom we have emotionally "bonded," while our fiduciary responsibilities dictated that we worked for someone for whom we had no feelings at all. These conflicting feelings often occurred when we worked in subagency relationships. Due to these conflicts as well as consumer and legislative efforts, today real estate practitioners are more candid about their relationships to buyers and sellers. Sales practitioners also may offer more agency and nonagency choices to consumers.

Because many questions stem from our agency relationships with buyers and sellers, it is helpful to understand the differences between working *for clients* rather than *with customers*. We must also examine the various agency and non-agency relationships possible in today's marketplace.

Differences Between Clients and Customers

Individuals who employ the services of a broker are called clients. (However, the client is not necessarily the person who pays the agent. For example, most buyers' agents are actually paid a commission by the seller.) Clients can also be called *principals* or *employers*. Brokers have a fiduciary relationship with clients and are obligated to give them loyalty and confidentiality. Brokers are advocates for their clients, and as such, owe them the highest degree of care, skill, and diligence. Everything brokers know about the property that is material to the transaction must be revealed to their clients.

Traditionally, the seller has employed real estate agents. In that role, the practitioner's objective is to obtain the best possible price and terms for the seller from a buyer. For example, a real estate agent representing the seller would inform the buyer about the prospective purchase but would not act as an advocate for the buyer. Seller agents would also seek the largest binder deposit possible from the buyer. If the buyer were the client, then the agent would advise the buyer on how to obtain the property for the lowest price and with terms most favorable to the buyer—for example, suggesting a minimal deposit.

Brokers work with but do not represent customers. While brokers do not have a fiduciary relationship with customers, nevertheless they owe them good faith, honesty, and expertise. Customers can also expect that brokers will disclose facts on the condition of property and other material informa-

Figure 7.1	Agent's duties/responsibilities to the client and the customer.

| **Client** ◄——— **AGENT** ———► **Customer** | |
| *Client-Level (Fiduciary) Services* | *Customer-Level Services* |

Client-Level (Fiduciary) Services	Customer-Level Services
1. Salesperson works *for* client	1. Salesperson works *with* customer
2. Loyalty (good faith)	2. Good faith
3. Confidentiality	3. Honesty
4. Full disclosure	4. Disclosure of facts/property condition
5. Obedience	5. Good service
6. Accounting for all aspects of transaction	6. Accounting for escrow funds
7. Care, skill, and diligence	7. Reasonable care, skill, and diligence
8. Advice	8. Information
9. Advocacy	9. No advocacy
10. Relationship based on highest degree of trust and confidence	10. Relationship based on ordinary degree of trust and confidence

tion. Buyers traditionally have been in the role of customers, not clients. However, with the public's rising awareness about the various roles a real estate agent can play, many buyers are now insisting on representation.

Agency and Nonagency Relationships

Brokers today must consider offering buyers representation as well as a number of alternative relationships with sellers and buyers.

- *Seller's broker.* In this type of brokerage, the firm represents sellers and never buyers. Seller brokerage firms encourage their agents to get listings. While seller brokerage firms work *with* buyers, they never work *for* buyers. As buyers are always customers and never clients, they can expect honesty and information but never advice or confidentiality. Sellers' brokers must disclose their relationship to buyers. Buyers should then be offered options: they can choose to remain unrepresented or they can choose another broker or attorney to represent them. Some firms practice *subagency* when they cooperate with other brokers and their clients. Subagency is typically practiced by licensees who show a cooperative firm's listing to a buyer when the buyer chooses not to be represented. Once a common practice, subagency is on the wane since it often leads to undisclosed dual agency, an illegal and unethical relationship.

- *Buyer's broker.* In this form of brokerage, the firm represents only buyers. This firm never takes employment (listings) from sellers. Sellers are treated as customers and buyers are treated as clients. Buyer brokers negotiate the best possible price and terms for their buyers.

Seller's Broker	Buyer's Broker
Works *for* the seller and obtains best price and terms for the seller while working *with* buyers.	Works *for* the buyer and obtains the lowest price and best terms for the buyer while working *with* sellers.
Buyers are offered information and expertise but no advice.	Sellers are offered information and expertise but no advice.

- *Single-agency broker.* The single-agency firm represents only one side in any given transaction: *either* the seller *or* the buyer. The single-agency broker never represents both buyer and seller in the same transaction. The advantage of this approach for brokers and consumers is that this agency's consumer is always treated as a client or principal. If consumers want to sell their property, the single agency brokerage can represent them. When the same consumers want to buy property, the same brokerage firm can represent them.
- *Dual-agency broker.* The dual-agency broker represents *both* the buyer *and* the seller in the same transaction. Dual agency requires written, informed consent to be legal. Dual agency can happen accidentally due to lack of proper disclosure—for example, if a seller's broker allows a buyer to make and share confidential information (such as negotiating strategy) without clearly warning the buyer of the broker's agency relationship with the seller. Accidental dual agency is unlawful; in some states all forms of dual agency, informed or accidental, are illegal.

Single-Agency Broker	Dual-Agency Broker
Represents buyers *or* sellers but not both in the same transaction	Represents buyers *and* sellers in the same transaction. - legal with informed consent in most states - illegal without informed consent

- *Legal dual agency.* In this relationship, both parties are aware that the broker is representing both sides to get the best price and terms for all parties. In many states, dual agency is legal only with written, informed consent. In the past, the NAR, most practitioners, and state regulatory agencies cautioned against dual agency. However, the NAR now considers disclosed dual agency a viable alternative, and numerous states have recognized it through legislation as a legitimate brokerage relationship.

- *Illegal dual agency.* In this relationship, one or both parties are unaware that the broker is representing both parties. Illegal dual agency is likely to occur when agency disclosure was not made or was made improperly. This type of agency is likely to occur on in-house sales (where listing agents have an incentive to sell their own listings) and in subagency relationships (where the selling agent is working closely with a buyer but has an employment contract through the listing broker to work for the seller).

- *Designated (dual) agency.* This form of lawful dual agency permits the brokerage firm to assign one licensee from the firm to represent the seller and another licensee to represent the buyer. Even though the firm still acts as a dual agent, the buyer and seller should be able to receive a higher level of advocacy than if one licensee had represented both the buyer and seller.

- *Facilitator.* This is a relatively new form of brokerage where the real estate practitioner represents *neither* the buyer *nor* the seller. The real estate practitioner brings the parties together and acts as a conduit through which offers and information are passed back and forth. Facilitators do not have a fiduciary relationship with buyers or sellers. Facilitators are also called *mediators* or *transaction brokers.*

Many excellent books explore various agency relationships in depth, including discussion regarding compensation and disclosure. See the appendix for a list of some of these books.

Lawsuits Concerning Agency Representation

Real estate practitioners received a clarion call to improve their agency disclosure practice in the landmark 1993 Edina Realty lawsuit. A homebuyer who worked with an Edina agent sued the Minneapolis, Minnesota, brokerage, one of the largest independent realty firms in the nation. The buyer alleged that dual agency relationships were not explained to her when she bought a home that Edina listed. The $210 million state court class action lawsuit charged Edina Realty with fraud, breach of fiduciary duty, breach of contract, and violation of racketeering statutes. The federal lawsuit could have jeopardized as much as $200 million in commissions from more than 6,000 transactions.

Sellers who argued that they were not fully apprised of the various agency relationships involved in a transaction filed a second class action suit against Edina for $75 million. The parties to the lawsuits settled in early 1994. The plaintiffs accepted a settlement whereby they received discounted future services from Edina Realty. In addition, Edina was ordered to make a donation to an undisclosed charity and to pay for all court costs. A federal lawsuit against Edina which alleged five counts of wrongdoing including racketeering was settled in late 1994.

The Edina Realty lawsuit demonstrates that it is best to establish a policy regarding what type of agency representation a brokerage firm will practice and to disclose that representation to all parties early in the relationship. In a Gallup survey commissioned by the National Association of REALTORS® 65 percent of surveyed buyers said they were told *at the first meeting,* or already knew, who the agent represented. Even if state law permits brokers and agents to disclose representation late in the relationship with consumers, it is not a good idea to delay: waiting creates an enhanced possibility of dual agency, as buyers and sellers begin to trust the real estate agent early in the relationship. Agents never really know when that trust is placed in them, but that trust is the beginning of an agency relationship. An agency

Sample Agency Disclosure to a Buyer/Customer

As a prospective purchaser/renter, you should know that the listing and cooperating (selling) real estate broker and associates are the agents of the seller/lessor and will be paid for their services by the seller/lessor, except as otherwise agreed in writing by the broker, seller/lessor, and the purchaser/renter. A broker and associate representing the seller can

1. Provide you with information on available properties and sources of financing
2. Show you available properties and describe their attributes and amenities
3. Assist you in submitting an offer to purchase/lease

The law obligates the listing broker, the cooperating broker (acting as subagent), and their sales agents to treat you honestly and in good faith. They must

1. Present all offers to the seller promptly
2. Respond honestly and accurately to questions concerning the property
3. Disclose any latent defects about the property of which the broker is aware

Sample Disclosure for Buyer Representation

If you are interested in buying real property, you can engage a real estate agent as a buyer's representative. A buyer's agent acts solely on behalf of the buyer. You can authorize a buyer's agent to do other things, including working with seller's agents on a cooperative basis.

A buyer's agent has the following fiduciary duties: reasonable care, undivided loyalty, full disclosure, confidentiality, obedience, and a duty to account.

In dealings with the seller, a buyer's agent should exercise reasonable skill and performance of duties; deal honestly, fairly, and in good faith; and disclose all facts known to the agent materially affecting the buyer's ability and/or willingness to perform a contract to acquire seller's property that are not inconsistent with the agent's fiduciary duties to buyer.

Adapted from the State of New York disclosure form used in residential transactions.

CASE STUDY 7.1   Culver v. Jaoudi

In a 1991 California Court Appeal decision in *Culver v. Jaoudi* (1 Cal. Rptr. 2d 680), a judge decided against the award of a commission to a broker who had failed to tell the seller that he was representing the buyer.

The broker had a buyer/client who was looking for a parcel of land to develop. The broker contacted an owner who had a parcel for sale. The broker asked for a one-time listing from the seller, who agreed to pay a 3 percent commission if a buyer could be found.

The broker presented the seller with his buyer/client's offer, and after negotiation, the buyer and seller agreed upon a sale price. At closing, the sale was consummated, but the seller refused to pay the $52,500 commission to the broker for failure to disclose that he was representing the buyer in the transaction. The broker sued.

The judge ruled against the broker, saying, "The agent has a fiduciary duty to his principal to disclose all information in the agent's possession relevant to the subject matter of the agency." The broker was representing both the buyer and the seller, and in this case, the dual agency must be clearly disclosed to both parties. Since the broker failed to tell the seller that he was representing the buyer, the penalty for failure to disclose the dual representation is loss of the sales commission.

"Who do I work for? I can't even remember what I work for!"

relationship can form unintentionally, as it does not necessarily begin with the signing of an employment contract but can be construed from our actions. For that reason, agents must provide buyers and sellers with all the information necessary for them to decide how much trust they wish to place in them.

The debate over agency representation is heated. NAR members, MLS subscribers, and the public all have vested interests in the argument because it affects compensation, cooperation among agents, liability, and service to customers and clients. Because newer forms of agency representation are evolving, real estate practitioners must cope with increasingly complex questions from real estate consumers. Many of these questions pose ethical concerns.

Exercise	How Would YOU Respond?

Using the models for ethical decision making suggested in earlier chapters, respond to these questions. Possible responses are provided at the end of the chapter.

1. If I work for the sellers, but I want the buyers to trust me enough to develop an offer, what should I say if the buyers ask me, "Who do you work for?"

_____

_____

_____

2. What should I do if the buyers want me to represent them as well as the sellers?

_____

_____

_____

3. If I work for the sellers, what should I say if the buyers ask me, "What price will the sellers take on this property?"

_____

_____

_____

4. If I work for the sellers, what should I say if the buyers ask me, "Have the sellers had any offers? What were they?" or "What did the sellers pay for their house?"

_____

_____

_____

5. The sellers' property has a design flaw: the family room faces due west. In the afternoon, that part of the house is like an oven. If I work for the sellers, should I disclose this defect to buyers?

_____

_____

_____

6. I work for the buyers. They want to make offers on a property where the seller is willing to hold paper. They have told me in confidence that their credit history had some blemishes on it, but the problems were resolved several years ago. Am I obligated to tell prospective sellers about those past problems?

_____

_____

_____

7. I work for the buyers. They have asked my advice about how much money to provide as a binder or earnest money deposit on this contract. I know that the more money they put up, the more likely the sellers are to go through with this transaction. But the more money they put up, the more risk there is for them. What should I do?

_____

_____

_____

8. I work for the buyers. Whenever I make appointments with cobrokers to show their listings, I advise those brokers up front that I am a buyer broker. In addition to revealing fiduciary information in their MLS brochures, they also share confidential fiduciary information with me over the phone. Since I clearly disclosed to the cobrokers that I was not working for their seller, may I now reveal the fiduciary information to my buyers?

_____

_____

_____

9. My firm has taken a listing on a commercial property. One of my family members is interested in making an offer. May I represent my family when my firm works for the seller?

_____

_____

_____

10. I work for the sellers and have completed a thorough market analysis for them. If the buyers ask to see it, may I give them the information?

_____

_____

_____

11. A potential listing client confided that she is in grave financial circumstances and must sell quickly. She listed her property with a competi-

tor. Now I am working with a buyer-client who has expressed interest in that seller's property. Should I tell my buyer about the seller's reasons for selling?

---

12. My commercial landlord-client has shopping center space for lease. I know that the two major department stores that anchor the center will be leaving in three months. What should I tell interested tenant-customers?

Possible Responses

1. *If I work for the seller, but I want the buyers to trust me enough to develop an offer, what should I say if the buyers ask me, "Who do you work for?"*

   If you work for the seller, you might respond at the earliest opportunity: "I represent the sellers. This means that I market their home and try to get the best price and terms for it. I can assist you with answering questions about the home and the neighborhood as well as with obtaining financing. I cannot advise you about what to offer, though. If you are interested in making an offer on the home, I will submit it to the sellers for their consideration."

   Check your state's laws about written disclosure forms that you may have to provide to the buyer. In some states, buyers have to sign a form indicating they have been given informed consent about agency representation.

2. *What should I do if the buyers want me to represent them as well as the sellers?*

   If the sellers have already employed you, you might respond: "I would have to discuss this matter with my broker and the sellers. Generally, dual agency is a difficult position for an agent to be in because it means representing two adverse parties. But with your permission and the permission of the sellers, it may be possible."

Avoid this dual agency situation if possible. Even though dual agency is legal with the proper disclosure and consent, you walk a legal tightrope when you represent parties with opposite interests. If you choose to become a dual agent, obtain written permission from both parties and seek legal guidance yourself.

In some states, you can offer designated dual agency as an option to the buyer and seller. Consult with your broker to determine which office associate will be assigned to one of your clients and discuss the implications of this arrangement with your buyer, seller, and office associate.

If you are a cooperating agent acting as a subagent you might respond: "I represent the sellers, even though I have not met them. The sellers will pay their listing broker a professional fee that my firm shares, so I work to get them the best price and terms for their home. That means I cannot represent you if I act in this capacity. However, I can still show you a wide selection of properties, offer you my expertise in obtaining financing, and give you information about the property and the neighborhood. I cannot offer you advice on what price or terms to offer."

If you are in the relatively early stages of your relationship with the buyer and you have discussed buyer agency with your broker, you can give buyers a choice regarding representation and choose to become a buyer broker: "If you would like me to represent you, that can be arranged. Then I can offer you advice instead of mere information. I would try to get you the property at the lowest price and best terms for you."

Another possible response to buyers and sellers is to suggest facilitation (if the broker approves and if it does not violate state law): "I can act as an agent for the seller (through subagency); I can act as your agent as well as the seller's agent (dual agency); or I can represent neither you nor the seller (facilitation), if you prefer. If you choose the third option, I can bring the parties together and act as a mediator. I will not offer advice to either party, which you can receive from your attorney or other advisers."

Remember, if the sellers have already employed you as their listing agent, you have a duty to represent them. You may not enter into a representation or a facilitation agreement with the buyers without the seller's express understanding and agreement.

3. *If I work for the sellers, what should I say if the buyers ask me, "What price will the sellers take on this property?"*

You might respond: "I know the seller will accept the listed price. I cannot quote you any other price. However, I must submit any offer you would like to make and the seller will make the final decision on the price."

You should not reveal any other price or suggest a suitable initial offering price unless the seller has given those instructions. When you state, "I must submit all offers," you have indicated that the price and terms may be negotiable. You should not indicate anything more.

4. *If I work for the sellers, what should I say if the buyers ask me, "Have the sellers had any offers? What were they?" or "What did the sellers pay for the house?"*

This information is strictly confidential unless the sellers give you permission to reveal it. You might respond, "Since I represent the sellers and I am trying to get them the best price and terms, I cannot disclose that information. However, I will be happy to submit any offer you would like to extend to the sellers." The price that the sellers paid for the property is a matter of public record in most cases. Because the buyers can find that information on their own, you may decide to keep that information proprietary.

5. *The sellers' property has a design flaw: the family room faces due west. In the afternoon, that part of the house is like an oven. If I work for the sellers, should I disclose this defect to buyers?*

You may choose to show the property when it can be seen in its best light (no pun intended). However, you should also point out to the buyers that the rooms facing west may be very warm in the afternoon. If the buyers want to the see the home in the afternoon, you should show it to them. Because the home's orientation may be material to some buyers and not to others, the wisest course would be to disclose this design flaw.

6. *I work for the buyers. They want to make offers on property where the seller is willing to hold paper. They have told me in confidence that their credit history had some blemishes on it, but the problems were resolved several years ago. Am I obligated to tell prospective sellers about those past problems?*

Yes, though you have a fiduciary responsibility to the buyer, you may not be dishonest with the sellers. You may wish to advise the buyers that concealing information about their credit could risk a lawsuit later. You should also consider working with them to present their case fairly: help the buyers obtain information (audited tax returns, credit reports) to help the sellers intelligently decide about providing financing.

7. *I work for the buyers. They have asked my advice about how much money to provide as a binder or earnest money deposit on this contract. I know that the more money they put up, the more likely the sellers are to go through with this transaction. But the more money they put up, the more risk there is for them. What should I do?*

Since you work for the buyers, you should obtain the best terms for them. Your concern over the ultimate consummation of this sale and your receipt of commission should be secondary to your clients' interests. However, to offset your concerns about the closing of the sale, you might suggest that you be paid a nonrefundable retainer for your services credited to the total fee due upon closing. You should also advise the buyers that a larger deposit may make their offer more persuasive to the sellers, if that is the case.

8. *I work for the buyers. Whenever I make appointments with cobrokers to show their listings, I advise those brokers up front that I am a buyer broker. In addition to revealing fiduciary information in their MLS brochures, they also share confidential fiduciary information with me over the phone. Since I clearly disclosed to the cobrokers that I was not working for their seller, may I now reveal the fiduciary information to my buyers?*

If you are absolutely sure that you disclosed to the listing broker that you are not working for them and their client, and the listing broker shares confidential information with you, you should still remind the broker at every opportunity that information you gather about the property must be given to your clients, the buyers.

9. *My firm has taken a listing on a commercial property. One of my family members is interested in making an offer. May I represent my family when my firm works for the seller?*

First, this situation can occur whether the property is commercial, residential, or other kinds of real estate. It is not uncommon for brokers or their agents to develop a personal interest in one of their own listings. However, the sellers have already employed you to represent them, and you may have gleaned confidential information about the property and the terms for sale. It might be best to release the listing you have with the sellers (upon your broker's permission), advising them that a conflict of interest has arisen. Even if the sellers agree to release the listing, you may not share fiduciary information with your family members unless given permission to do so. The sellers may be willing to accept a dual agency or facilitation arrangement. However, the sellers may be at a disadvantage in either of those relationships because of what you know. Another possibility is not only to release the listing but to suggest to your family members that they select another firm. You will not create a dual agency situation if you keep the listing and send your relatives to another broker.

10. *I work for the sellers and have completed a thorough market analysis for them. If the buyers ask to see it, may I give them the information?*

The information you gave to the sellers belongs to them and is proprietary. They pay you a commission if the property sells, a payment that reimburses you for the marketing of their real estate. You may ask them for permission to show those specific comparables to buyers, or you can show the buyers other comparables. You can also share public information with interested buyers by providing statistics about properties that have sold in the area. This information should give the buyers what they need to know to make an informed offer on your listing and not compromise your position with the sellers.

11. *A potential listing client confided that she is in grave financial circumstances and must sell quickly. She listed her property with a competitor. Now I am working with a buyer-client who has expressed interest in that seller's property. Should I tell my buyer about the seller's reasons for selling?*

Bruce Aydt, chair of NAR's Professional Standards Committee, suggests that sellers should be told that information won't be held confidential until a listing is signed. If the seller hasn't been warned, then real estate practitioners should keep the information confidential. If the seller has been warned and discloses personal information anyway, then the agent can give the buyer-client the information. (See "I've Got A Secret—Do I Tell?" in *REALTOR,* May, 1999, p. 50.)

12. *My commercial landlord-client has shopping center space for lease. I know that the two major department stores that anchor the center will be leaving in three months. What should I tell interested tenant-customers?*

No doubt the commercial landlord would prefer to keep this information confidential, not only because it would create issues regarding attracting tenants but also it would possibly deter existing tenants from renewing their leases. However, this information is material and relevant to any commercial tenant contemplating establishing a business in this center. Most small businesses in shopping centers derive a substantial part of their income from shoppers visiting larger department stores. Discuss with the landlord the possibility of doing short-term leases with options to renew for any new tenants and work vigorously to find new anchor tenants. When discussing mall space for rent, you have to disclose this information to prospective tenants.

Applying Ethics:
Fair Housing

"Isn't it wonderful that we don't have to wait a single moment to improve the world?"

Anne Frank

The civil rights of home buyers are legally protected by the federal 1968 Fair Housing Act and a host of state and local laws. Despite these laws, minorities seeking to buy or rent a home still experience discrimination. The Department of Housing and Urban Development (HUD), the government agency that handles housing discrimination, received 10,000 complaints in 1997 alone. Since 1988, HUD has been given increased latitude to enforce fair housing laws that have been in place for over a quarter of a century.

Real estate practitioners have a special mandate to ensure that all buyers and renters are treated fairly. The Civil Rights Acts of 1866 and 1968 allow no practitioner to discriminate in residential sales or leasing based on race, color, religion, national origin, gender, handicap, or family status. Some state and local ordinances have added more protected classes, such as marital status and sexual orientation. Real estate firms that violate federal, state, or local civil rights statutes can lose their operating licenses and be heavily fined as well.

The Fair Housing Act

The Federal Fair Housing Act, Title VIII of the Civil Rights Act of 1968, is a comprehensive and modern housing law, establishing, within constitutional limits, the basis for fair housing throughout the U.S. In 1968, it covered discriminatory practices based on race, religion, or national origin. In 1974, it was amended to include gender. The Fair Housing Amendments Act of 1988, which took effect on March 12, 1989, added two new protected classes of persons to the Fair Housing Act:

1. A handicapped individual who is defined as being a person with a physical or mental impairment that substantially limits one or more major life activities
2. Family status, which is defined as persons under age 18 living with a parent or guardian (in other words, discrimination against children)

There are two limitations on these new classes as well:

1. Housing and apartment complexes designed for senior citizens and complexes that are at least 80 percent occupied by one person per unit age 55 or older
2. State and local occupancy legislation that can still be imposed upon dwelling and apartments (if state or local occupancy laws would allow two adults in an apartment, they would also have to allow an adult and a child)

There are also criminal provisions to the Federal Fair Housing Act that cover intimidation, coercion, or threats made by brokers, salespersons, and owners against people trying to obtain fair housing rights. For example, if an African-American family moves into a Caucasian neighborhood and the family's home is firebombed, the FBI will investigate as this is a federal crime.

Headlines

Chicago Landlord Pays $180,000 for Sexual Harassment

Handicapped San Jose Resident Wins $126,000 Over Broken Elevator

Cupertino Mother Gets $40,000 in Family Settlement

Atlantic City Landlord to Pay $25,000 for Sexual Harassment and Retaliation Against Hispanics

From *National Fair Housing Advocate*, Vol. 5, No. 3, April 1995.

Racial Discrimination

HUD reported that race continues to be the greatest single factor in housing discrimination, named in more than 50 percent of the cases filed. Complainants charged they were frequently told different terms and conditions of rental, faced with eviction, and often were the targets of racial epithets.

From "ALQ Updates." January 1992. Agency Law Quarterly, 3:92.

The average rejection ratio for African-Americans who attempt to obtain home loans is 2:1, meaning that for every Caucasian who is rejected, two African-Americans are rejected. The city with the worst ratio is Minneapolis with a ratio of 2.96:1.

Adapted from *Palm Beach Post*, "Blacks get fewer mortgages than whites." 2 January 1995, p. 4B.

CASE STUDY 8.1   Civil Rights and the Broker

An Atlanta real estate broker is at the center of the first civil rights case in the U.S. taken before an administrative law judge as authorized by the 1988 amendments to the Fair Housing Act.

Gordon Blackwell, a broker in Stone Mountain, Georgia, listed a home he owned through a Coldwell Banker firm in April 1989. In May and June, an African American couple assisted by a Re/Max practitioner entered into negotiation for the property and reached an agreement. After the contract was signed, but before closing, Blackwell learned that the couple was African American and advised his agent that he would not close. At the time, he argued that he was not aware of contract clauses that required him to pay points and closing costs.

A few days before closing, Blackwell called the agent and stated that he had rented the house to a white couple.

The Re/Max practitioner and the buyers filed a complaint with the Atlanta office of HUD, which brought charges against Blackwell. The judge found Blackwell guilty and ordered him to pay about $75,000 in fines and penalties and to close on the house.

Blackwell filed for bankruptcy and the mortgagee foreclosed on the home before the black couple could take ownership. The federal government filed an injunction against the mortgagee to refrain from selling the home.

The Georgia Real Estate Commission revoked Blackwell's real estate license.

Most buyers and sellers are aware of civil rights legislation. Some are personally opposed to integration or have other political sentiments that contradict fair housing laws. Brokers and their employees may also have personal feelings in conflict with civil rights legislation. These concerns can create ethical dilemmas for real estate practitioners. Consider case studies 8.1 (previous page) through 8.4.

CASE STUDY 8.2   Civil Rights and the Developer

An African-American couple in Chicago filed suit against a home developer when the developer refused to sell a house to the couple after they had made an offer and put down a deposit. The developer's sales agent notified the couple of the developer's alleged housing discrimination after he was told by the developer to discourage the couple because of their race. The sales agent and a Chicago fair housing organization joined with the couple to file the lawsuit. The developer agreed to a $935,000 out-of-court settlement, but did not admit any wrongdoing.

Adapted from "Legal Briefs," *Realtor News*, September 26, 1994, p. 4.

CASE STUDY 8.3   Subfranchisee Found Guilty

Century 21 Real Estate has been held liable for race discrimination practices by a subfranchisee, even though the company had no franchise agreement with the guilty party. In *Payne v. Weber Realty* (Pennsylvania Court of Common Pleas, First District, No. 2260) a jury found Weber Realty of Philadelphia guilty of refusing to show homes in white neighborhoods to an African-American who filed suit under state civil rights laws.

Weber is a franchisee of Century 21 of Eastern Pennsylvania, which is a franchisee of the Century 21 Real Estate Corporation. Century 21 of Eastern Pennsylvania was not named in the lawsuit.

This case is considered a landmark because real estate franchisors have traditionally won this type of case. State real estate licensing laws don't allow franchisors as much control, according to a franchise magazine. But the state judge ruled that Century 21 was liable and fined them $40,000 in punitive damages. The Weber firm and its sales associates were also ordered to pay the prospective buyer $160,000 in compensatory and punitive damages.

Many real estate practitioners and members of the public misunderstand the practitioner's responsibility toward civil rights. The Civil Rights Act does not require that real estate practitioners integrate neighborhoods. The purpose of the Civil Rights Act is to give everyone a chance to buy an affordable home, regardless of ethnicity, race, religion, gender, national origin, handicap, or family status. Practitioners can legally use no form of discrimination other than discriminating against inability to afford a home. It is their legal and ethical responsibility to be an advocate of fair housing and to give everyone an equal opportunity to enjoy the American dream of home ownership.

CASE STUDY 8.4 | **Moving Out**

A white couple agreed to sell their home to settle a $10 million lawsuit accusing the family of harassing their next door neighbors with racial slurs and death threats. The neighbors who filed the federal civil rights lawsuit are a Chicago police officer of African-American and Puerto Rican descent and his Puerto Rican wife.

The white couple, John and Marie Kraft, had lived in their northwest side home for 20 years. Isidor and Minerva Ramos had lived there for over nine years. The lawsuit alleged that within a year, the Krafts, their three children, and a son-in-law began hurling racial insults and obscenities at the Ramos family. The harassment eventually escalated to death threats, the lawsuit claimed.

The U.S. District judge told both families to "Get over it and move on" when the settlement was reached.

Adapted from "White Couple to Sell Home to Settle Racial Bias Lawsuit," *Palm Beach Post,* 3 January 1994, p. 24 A.

What Constitutes Discrimination in the Sale or Rental of Housing?

1. Refusing to sell or rent after a bona fide offer has been made or refusing to negotiate for the sale or rental of, or otherwise make unavailable or deny, a dwelling to any person because of race, color, religion, national origin, gender, handicap, or family status

2. Discriminating against any person in the terms, conditions, or privileges of sale or rental of a dwelling, or in the provision of services or facilities in connection therewith, because of race, color, religion, national origin, gender, handicap, or family status

(continued)

What Constitutes Discrimination?   Continued.

3. Making, printing, or publishing or causing to be made, printed, or published any notice, statement, or advertisement with respect to the sale or rental of a dwelling that indicates any preference, limitation, or discrimination based or race, color, religion, national origin, gender, handicap, or family status, or an intention to make any such preference, limitation, or discrimination

4. Representing to any person because of race, color, religion, national origin, gender, handicap, or family status that any dwelling is not available for inspection, sale, or rental when such dwelling is in fact so available

5. For profit, inducing or attempting to induce any person to sell or rent any dwelling by representation regarding the entry or prospective entry into the neighborhood of a person or persons of a particular race, color, religion, national origin, gender, handicap, or family status

Exercise   How Would YOU Respond?

Using the models for ethical decision making suggested in earlier chapters, respond to these questions. Possible responses are provided at the end of the chapter.

1. My sellers refuse to sell to certain minority groups. What should I tell them?

2. My sellers may say, "I can market my home by myself and not have to worry about whom I sell to!"

3. My sellers may say, "I can go to another broker who feels differently about this!"

_____

_____

_____

4. My listing client is a condominium homeowner. He told me that his apartment can only be sold to older people.

_____

_____

_____

5. After I showed an apartment to my customer, the manager called me to say that he would not rent the unit to her because she was handicapped. He said he didn't want to depress the other tenants. What should I do?

_____

_____

_____

6. My client is a landlord who charges a higher security deposit to male tenants than to female tenants because she believes males are messier than females. She wants me to handle the rental listing on all her properties and to enforce her security deposit policies. What should I do?

_____

_____

_____

7. What if my buyers ask, "I know you can't tell me, but what kind of people live in the neighborhood?"

_____

_____

_____

8. What if my buyers persist by asking, "But will I be comfortable living here?"

_____

_____

_____

9. What if my buyers say, "I belong to a particular religious group (or ethnic group), and I want to be with people of my own kind"? May I assist these buyers?

_____

_____

_____

10. What if my buyers say, "We want to live within one mile of our synagogue/church"? May I assist these buyers?

_____

_____

_____

11. What if I know of incidents of racial hatred in the neighborhood? Should I disclose this information to my minority buyers?

_____

_____

_____

Questions about crime in a neighborhood may also lead real estate practitioners into troubled waters. Customer questions about crime can be a subtle way of asking about the ethnic makeup of an area. Respond to these questions.

12. What if my buyer asks, "Is there crime in this neighborhood?"

_____

_____

_____

13. What if I know the sellers are selling their home because they were robbed and assaulted there?

_____

_____

_____

It is understandable that parents with school-age children want to know about the quality of the schools, but these questions can also be a way of obtaining information regarding racial or ethnic balance of a neighborhood. Respond to this question.

14. My buyers ask, "How are the schools in this area? What kind of children attend the schools?"

_____

_____

_____

Discrimination can also take place within the real estate office itself. Respond to this question.

15. I've noticed that real estate practitioners in my firm are relatively inconsistent in the way they treat customers. Although all buyers are treated courteously, I notice that well-dressed customers are not asked as many questions about finances as less well-dressed customers. Younger people are always asked about whether commuting distance to work is a factor and older people aren't. Are these problems?

_____

_____

_____

16. I'm a broker. How can I convince my agents to practice fair housing when I believe that we all harbor some prejudices?

_____

_____

_____

Possible Responses

1. *My sellers refuse to sell to certain minority groups. What should I tell them?*

   First, address the legal issue: "Mr. and Mrs. Seller, the Civil Rights Act of 1968 prohibits me from marketing your home based on a buyer's race (or religion, etc). No real estate broker can market your home on that basis."

   Next, address the marketing issue: "If I were to follow your instructions, I would be limiting the number of people who could afford your home, and in today's market, any kind of buying restriction would increase the time it takes to sell your home."

   If the sellers insist: "I cannot take this listing under these circumstances. Please understand that any buyers who feel discriminated against on the basis of their race (or religion, etc.) could file charges with HUD against you and my company. It is not worth taking your listing if I lose my real estate license or see you in court facing a $100,000 fine."

2. *My sellers may say, "But I can market my home by myself and not have to worry about whom I sell to!"*

   You can respond by saying, "That's only partially true. The Fair Housing Act does exempt owners of single-family homes subject to certain conditions: the owner may not own or have an interest in more than three such houses at any one time. In the case of a single-family home in which the owner was not the most recent occupant prior to its sale, the owner may not have made any other such sale within the preceding 24 months. The unit must be sold or rented without the use of a real estate broker or agent and without the use of any discriminatory advertisement. Furthermore, under no circumstance can you discriminate on the basis of race. You may have some exemptions regarding other protected classes.

3. *My sellers may say, "I can go to another broker who feels differently about this!"*

   You should respond, "No broker can legally assist you in discrimination. You and that broker will risk facing a lawsuit."

4. *My listing client is a condominium homeowner. He told me that his apartment can only be sold to older people.*

   There are exceptions to the Civil Rights Amendment of 1988 dealing with family status and children. These exceptions are very narrow, however. Ask your condominium owner: "Are 100 percent of the occupants of this condominium complex 62 years old or more or are at least 80 percent 55 years old? Does your complex have special facilities designed for the elderly? Does your condominium have clearly published guidelines to this effect?"

All advertising done on behalf of this condominium seller must state that the unit is available only to older persons. Do not take the seller's word that his complex is exempt from the 1988 Civil Rights Amendment regarding family status and age. Very few condominium complexes are exempt.

You may have to remind your sellers that the only color a real estate practitioner can see in this business is green—the color of money. In other words, how much cash do the buyers have? Can they afford to buy a home in this neighborhood? A practitioner can legally use no form of discrimination other than discriminating against inability to afford a home.

5. *After I showed an apartment to my customer, the manager called me to say that he would not rent the unit to her because she was handicapped. He said he didn't want to depress the other tenants. What should I do?*

Under the 1988 amendments to the Fair Housing Act, people with handicaps are a protected class. Under the law, the manager or owner is not obligated to rent to someone who would be a threat to the health and safety of others. The reaction of others to a handicapped person, however, is not a threat, nor is it the handicapped person's responsibility. It is not your responsibility, either. You should advise the manager that he is violating the Civil Rights law and warn him of the possible consequences.

Under the Fair Housing Act it is also illegal for a property manager to inquire about the nature of a person's handicap. A manager could deny a home or apartment to someone who is dangerous but is not allowed to ask questions that would determine if that individual is dangerous. A standard rental application form that provides references is one way managers can obtain this kind of information.

6. *My client is a landlord who charges a higher security deposit to male tenants than to female tenants because she believes males are messier than females. She wants me to handle the rental listing on all her properties and to enforce her security deposit policies. What should I do?*

Under the 1974 amendment to the Fair Housing Act, gender was declared a protected class. Treating tenants differently because of gender is illegal. You should advise the manager that she is violating the Civil Rights law and warn her of the possible consequences. If she persists, you should discuss with your broker the possibility of a release from the listing arrangement.

7. *What if my buyers ask, "I know you can't tell me, but what kind of people live in the neighborhood?"*

Your buyers are right. You cannot tell them what kind of people live in the neighborhood if they are asking you to characterize the neighborhood regarding the residents' race, color, religion, national origin, gender, age, handicap, or family status. However, you may respond: "The residents here are middle-class professionals," "The neighborhood is working class," or "The people here are upper income." You may describe the neighborhood in terms of its economics, but you cannot describe the neighborhood by the predominance of one ethnic, racial, or religious group, or of the color, gender, handicap, or family status of the residents.

Never use the expression, "This neighborhood is in transition." Never say, "The neighborhood is mixed" or "It's a salt-and-pepper area." The courts interpret these euphemisms as overtly discriminatory.

8. *What if my buyers persist by asking, "But will I be comfortable living here?"*

You may always respond, "I will be happy to show you any homes in this neighborhood in your budget, but if you want to know whether you will like living here, the best thing to do is to talk to the neighbors yourself." If you feel it is appropriate, drive around the neighborhood and perhaps introduce the buyers to the residents. You may also advise the buyers to drive through neighborhoods by themselves and choose neighborhoods they like, then show them houses they can afford in that neighborhood. You may want to give them specific addresses to drive by, but get permission from your broker first. Your broker may have a policy against giving out client addresses.

9. *What if my buyers say, "I belong to a particular religious group (or ethnic group), and I want to be with people of my own kind"? May I assist these buyers?*

Absolutely not. They are asking you to describe the neighborhood in terms of the residents' race or ethnicity. Again, you may describe neighborhoods only in terms of affordability and economics. Let the buyers decide for themselves which neighborhoods have the "right" kind of people.

You may tell the buyers: "I cannot describe the neighborhood in that fashion. However, if you want to ask your friends or relatives or members of your synagogue/church/parish where they live, I will be happy to show you homes in their neighborhoods that you can afford." Remember to always disavow any suggestion that you would help discriminate illegally and always return to the issue of economics and affordability.

10. *What if my buyers say, "We want to live within one mile of our synagogue/church"? May I assist these buyers?*

Of course. They are not asking you to choose homes in a particular ethnic neighborhood, but rather a neighborhood with a particular amenity. There is nothing wrong in helping these buyers, any more than assisting a buyer in finding a home near a bus stop or a grocery store.

11. *What if I know of incidents of racial hatred in the neighborhood? Should I disclose this information to my minority buyers?*

This question is a troublesome one. Are the incidents violent? Are members of racist groups burning crosses on lawns? Are neighbors hurling racial epithets? Even using racist language is a crime if used to intimidate prospective buyers. In a recent south Florida case, a neighbor was fined $1,000 for making loud, racist remarks while an agent was showing a home to an African-American prospect. (Also see the case of the Caucasian family forced to sell its home cited earlier in this chapter.)

There are two conflicting considerations here: on the one hand, you would not want to give the impression that you are trying to steer these customers by frightening them away from a neighborhood. On the other hand, withholding information that might be material to their purchase could be concealment.

There is no correct legal response, but you may wish to consider the ethics of the matter: if you were in your buyer's place, would you want to know that you might face overt racism in the neighborhood? Also, if you decide to advise African-American prospects about the potential danger, you should consider advising all prospects. Consult with your broker and the brokerage attorney and govern yourself appropriately.

12. *What if my buyer asks, "Is there crime in this neighborhood?"*

While there is probably crime in most American neighborhoods, chances are your buyer is concerned about particular kinds of crime—robbery, assault, and other violent activities. Nevertheless, it would be best not to answer this question unless you have current, specific information from the police or other informed sources.

You may wish to say: "I understand your concern about crime in the neighborhood. What kind of crime concerns you?" Then: "After we have looked at homes here, I will give you the phone number of the police department and you can speak with the neighborhood liaison officer." Always defer such questions to the professionals and experts who have the correct information.

13. *What if I know the sellers are selling their home because they were robbed and assaulted there?*

In some states, heinous crimes that occurred within three years of marketing the property must be revealed to prospective buyers. Barring such legislation, you must resolve conflicting demands. Your sellers probably want to keep the information about the robbery and assault confidential. Yet you can be sure the neighbors will tell the buyers about the crime as soon as they move in, so it is quite possible that the buyers could sue you for concealing this damaging information and win.

You may wish to ask the sellers for permission to reveal this information to prospective buyers. You and the seller may also gather statistics from the police about crime in the area and, if you find that this unfortunate incident was the exception and not the rule, you may be able to overcome any objection to the property by having such facts at your disposal. If the sellers deny permission, you may decide not to take the listing. Discuss this possibility with your broker first.

14. *My buyers ask, "How are the schools in this area? What kind of children attend the schools?"*

There are a number of problems in dealing with this question. For one, you may sell the buyers on a home because it is in a particular school district. What happens if next year, the school boundary lines change and that home now is served by another school? Ultimately, you may be liable.

Also, if you claim the schools are excellent, by what standards are you measuring those schools? Parents and educators have different standards by which they measure a school's excellence. For example, a parent of a teenage boy or girl might say that the school program is wonderful because the soccer team won first place in the state last year. Another parent might argue that sports are a minor factor in rating the school and that academic achievement is far more important. The age of the buyers' children and what the parents expect of the school program are closely related.

Rather than answer as an expert on the schools, defer to the experts—in this case, the buyers themselves. Direct your buyer toward the resources they need to evaluate the schools. Usually school boards publish an "Attendance Boundary Map Book," available at little or no cost. In addition, school boards have information about a school's accreditation, enrollment, procedures, transportation, and telephone contact numbers. Let the buyers research which schools offer the programs they want. At that point, they will have identified the neighborhood they wish to live in, and you can better satisfy their needs.

Remember, you should never characterize a school by saying, "The schools here are bad." The courts will interpret that remark as, "The schools here are integrated," a discriminatory and unacceptable remark. Again, refer the buyers to the experts on the school system: other parents, the school board, principals, teachers, and guidance counselors.

15. *I've noticed that real estate practitioners in my firm are relatively inconsistent in the way they treat customers. Although all buyers are treated courteously, I notice that well-dressed customers are not asked as many questions about finances as less well-dressed customers. Younger people*

are always asked about whether commuting distance to work is a factor and older people aren't. Are these problems?

They could become problems. Every buyer in your office should be treated in the same manner. Your office may want to create a list of information that they must gather from every buyer within a reasonable amount of time. This information might include property specifications (e.g., number of bedrooms and baths), financial considerations, and mortgage pre-qualification. If buyers have been prequalified, add that fact to their file. It is not important that every customer go through the buying process in the same sequence, but it might prevent a discrimination charge if you can demonstrate that every buyer provided the same information during the buying process.

16. *I'm a broker. How can I convince my agents to practice fair housing when I believe that we all harbor some prejudices?*

The purpose of fair housing laws is not to change people's hearts—although this is a noble goal. The purpose of these laws is to change people's conduct. REALTORS® recommend the following six guidelines:

1. Review your office policy on fair housing. Make sure you have procedures for:

   - how prospects are greeted at the office door;
   - how prospects are pre-qualified;
   - how properties are selected for showing (based on economic issues);
   - client/customer follow-up.

2. Adopt a procedure for immediately handling fair housing issues, such as questions, concerns, or complaints.

3. Conduct fair housing training sessions on a regular basis. Encourage associates to attend fair housing programs.

4. Do not tolerate jokes or stories regarding race, color, religion, gender, disabilities, national origin, or family status around the office.

5. Is your office accessible to disabled prospects? Is your fair housing poster prominently displayed?

6. Make sure your advertising describes the property and its amenities, not the "ideal" buyer or tenant.

Source: Adapted from *Florida REALTOR*, July/August, 1998, p. 25.

Applying Ethics:
Stigmatized Property

A growing number of states in the U.S. have adopted laws dealing with questions about stigmatized property. Most say real estate agents don't have to disclose such stigmas to buyers.

REALTOR® News

In recent years, television, movies, and other media have addressed the issue of properties stigmatized by death and violent crime. Perhaps The Amityville Horror was the first film to popularize the notion of a stigmatized property. While some real estate practitioners might shrug off these stories and headlines, many sellers insist that their agent keep their property's stigmas confidential. Buyers, on the other hand, claim they have the right to know how such a problem affects present and potential value.

Among the many problems that can stigmatize a property are crimes that have occurred on the property, a seller's illness (particularly AIDS), and real and suspected environmental hazards. About half the states have adopted laws regarding stigmatized property. Most laws do not require real estate agents to disclose such stigmas to buyers. What must be disclosed are matters that are "material" to the purchase.

The issue then becomes how to define "material." The courts have ruled that "material" information relates to the property's physical structure. Thus, buyers have a right to know about physical defects, such as leaky roofs and faulty equipment. However, a buyer may argue that anything that could affect resale value is material to the purchase; therefore the buyer has a right to know about nonstructural problems as well.

In many states, sellers must sign a latent defects disclosure similar to the one below, disclosing any information about the physical defects of a property.

Sample Disclosure of Latent Defects

Owner specifically acknowledges and understands that if Owner knows of latent defects materially affecting the value of the property, which are defects not readily observable, then Owner is under a duty to disclose said latent defects to the buyer. Owner represents that if Owner knows of said latent defects, they are set forth in writing under the "Special Clauses" provision below or in a written document attached to the listing contract. Owner shall notify Broker, in writing, of any latent defects that Owner becomes aware of during the term of this listing and any extension thereof. Owner authorizes Broker to disclose said latent defects to prospective purchasers.

Many sellers would be forthcoming about latent defects with or without mandatory disclosure laws. However, sellers may not wish to reveal information about nonphysical problems of the property. In the following example, consider whether the history of a property is a material fact. How can you determine the effect of a past history upon the market value of a home?

In a Florida case (see case study on page 45), buyers sued their real estate agent for not revealing a murder–suicide that took place on the property some months before closing. When the buyers found out about the tragedy, they stopped paying their mortgage, were foreclosed upon, and sued the agent for failure to disclose a material fact. This case raises the issue of the time frame of events that "psychologically impact" the property. Should an agent disclose "ancient history" as well as more recent events?

State laws regarding disclosure vary widely. Some states have no stigmatized property laws. Other states, such as California, decree that the agent must disclose any incident occurring within three years of an offer to buy, lease, or rent a property.

A more difficult question arises when the occupants are notorious rather than their home. For example, Charles Stuart of Boston gained notoriety when he murdered his pregnant wife and reported that a gunman had attacked him and his wife. Months later, when Stuart became implicated in the crime, he leapt from a bridge and killed himself. Before the Stuart home was sold in late 1990, the broker made full disclosure about the previous occupants, though Massachusetts law does not require disclosure and no death occurred there. The broker reported that only a few prospects refused to consider the home after hearing its history. The home sold at market price.

CASE STUDY 9.1	The Scene of the Crime

A short time after purchasing a $60,000 El Paso home, the buyer discovered that two owners earlier the house had been the site of a series of alleged but never proven child molestations. The buyer sued the broker, claiming the broker knew of the home's reputation. The jury ruled that the broker had breached his duty to disclose and had unfairly taken advantage of the buyer. The court awarded the buyer $220,000 in damages, closing costs, and mental anguish.

Sanchez v. Guerrero (1994 W.L. 373949 Tex. App. El Paso)

CASE STUDY 9.2	The Haunted House Case

The New York Supreme Court refused to order the return of a $32,500 down payment to Mr. and Mrs. Jeffrey Stambovsky, who wanted to leave their newly purchased $650,000 Rockland County home because they claimed it was inhabited by ghosts. According to the Stambovskys, the seller not only knew about the apparitions, she wrote about them in publications such as *Reader's Digest.* The court ruled that the seller did not have a duty to reveal her beliefs about supernatural inhabitants nor to discuss her published stories.

Adapted from "Skeletons in Closet Create Nightmare for Agents," *Miami Herald*, 31 October 1992.

Many buyers want to know about any psychological stigma attached to the property for reasons ranging from superstition to thinking they can get a better price on the property. The issue of AIDS as a potential psychological stigma is the most legally and ethically troubling. Confusion and hysteria about whether a buyer could become infected by living in the same house as an AIDS victim has resulted in some refusing to buy such homes. Some argue that a seller with AIDS is material, given the fear that some people have about transmission of AIDS through casual contact, although this fear has no scientific basis.

Real estate practitioners may find little relief in state law regarding disclosure of AIDS. While some state laws specifically state that real estate practitioners have no obligation to disclose that a property's occupant has AIDS, these laws also state that if asked, licensees must respond truthfully. It is advisable that if asked, the real estate practitioner respond along these lines: "I would prefer that you ask the owner (or property occupant) that question directly." HUD states that real estate brokers have no duty to investigate whether an occupant has AIDS and should avoid making such inquiries. Furthermore, HUD's general counsel advises that if agents are asked whether an occupant has AIDS, they should decline to respond.

Irrespective of state and federal statutes that govern the real estate agent's behavior and response in regard to stigmatized property, buyers continue to demand such information. While buyers have a right to seek answers on their own, they cannot expect real estate practitioners to provide them.

Exercise	How Would YOU Respond?

Using the models for ethical decision making suggested in earlier chapters, respond to these questions. Possible responses are provided at the end of the chapter.

1. What if my sellers tell me they are selling a recently inherited home because their uncle murdered his entire family and then committed suicide there?

2. What if the buyers ask me directly if the seller has AIDS?

3. What if I work for the buyers and have no fiduciary responsibility to keep the information about AIDS confidential? Under these circumstances, don't I have a duty to disclose this information to the buyers?

Possible Responses

1. What if my sellers tell me they are selling a recently inherited home because their uncle murdered his entire family and then committed suicide there?

Courts in many states have ruled that information about crimes taking place on the property is not material to the buyer and therefore need not be disclosed. About half of the states have laws that say buyers need not be told about psychological stigmas attached to properties, such as suicides and accidental deaths. However, some states, such as California, require that real estate practitioners discuss crimes that took place within three years of marketing the home.

Check with your broker's attorney regarding the legality of disclosing such information. If your state has no law mandating disclosure of information on a psychological stigma, consider discussing the matter with the seller: "Mr. and Mrs. Seller, you have told me about the death of your family on the property in confidence. I am bound by my fiduciary relationship with you to keep this matter confidential. While state law requires that I disclose latent defects and material information to the buyer, this matter falls into a gray area.

However, sooner or later the buyers of this property will find out about the tragedy. The neighbors across the street may tell them on moving day, and it may upset them greatly. I would prefer telling any prospective buyers what happened so they can decide early on whether it is an obstacle to the purchase. If we do not disclose and they are upset when they find out later, they may sue us for withholding information. You could be the test case for this state. Is that something you want to risk?

"Please release me from confidentiality (in writing) on this matter and allow me to tell buyers about the stigma attached to this property. Let them decide whether this affects their decision to purchase. This way, we can avoid litigation."

You may also advise your sellers to check with their attorney regarding their rights in this matter. If your sellers choose not to release the information, you may choose to refuse the listing after consulting with your broker.

2. What if the buyers ask me directly if the seller has AIDS?

As stated earlier, the federal government and many states have advised brokers and their agents not to offer this information. NAR suggests that if the buyer asks, the agent should state that the firm has a policy of not addressing that subject one way or the other. NAR also suggests that if buyers believe this information is important to their decision, they must pursue that investigation on their own.

3. *What if I work for the buyers and have no fiduciary responsibility to keep the information about AIDS confidential? Under these circumstances, don't I have a duty to disclose this information to the buyers?*

This question is more difficult to answer since the agent cannot rely on confidentiality. Fair housing laws are not clear on this matter either. Federal law does not stop a home buyer from using criteria that a seller is forbidden from using. Home buyers may exercise their freedom of choice and not violate the Fair Housing Act. The question here is whether you should provide the information to the buyer—should you be the one informing the buyer that the occupants have AIDS?

The best way to answer this question is to ask yourself if you would reveal the racial or ethnic composition of a neighborhood to a buyer if asked. Because providing this information could create an impression that you are steering buyers away from certain neighborhoods based on discriminatory factors, it would be unwise to do so. You may want to suggest that buyers who feel that this information is relevant can investigate on their own.

Applying Ethics: Environmental Hazards and Other Physical Defects

A man is ethical only when life, as such, is sacred to him, that of plants and animals as well as that of his fellow-man, and when he devotes himself fully to all life that is in need of help.

Albert Schweitzer

Due to the increasing awareness of environmental hazards, Congress passed a number of stringent regulations in the 1980s and early 1990s. These laws have had a major impact on real property and on real estate practitioners, not only legally but in terms of ethical obligations as well.

As a result of legislative mandates and social responsiveness, the 1990s are a decade of increased litigation on environmental hazards. "As is" contract clauses, the standard defense that sellers used in the past to hide property defects, are no longer viable. Neither is the principle of *caveat emptor:* "Let the buyer beware." The courts decree that sellers, lending institutions, and real estate agents are financially responsible to buyers for damages caused by environmental contaminants.

As an illustration, two important federal laws that regulate hazardous waste disposal are the Resource Conservation and Recovery Act (RCRA) and the Comprehensive Environmental Response, Compensation, and Liability Act (CERCLA, also known as Superfund), both administered by the Environmental Protection Agency (EPA). RCRA was designed to ensure that hazardous chemicals be disposed of properly so as not to harm human health or the environment. The Hazardous and Solid Waste amendments further strengthened RCRA, providing a "cradle to grave" responsibility for a list of 450 hazardous chemical wastes—a company is responsible for its waste from production to disposal. Thus, if a waste disposal firm illegally disposes of the waste, not only is the waste disposal company violating the law, so is the company that produced the waste in the first place.

Superfund allows the EPA to hold any company liable for the cost of the entire cleanup of an abandoned site, regardless of the amount of waste the company placed there. For example, if a company buys or a bank forecloses upon land that has been polluted, that company or bank is held responsible for the pollution even though someone else created the problem.

As a result of Superfund legislation, many banks and commercial buyers conduct thorough environmental audits prior to lending. Furthermore, they conduct extensive title searches to determine if the purchasers are innocent and to help avoid liability for any pollution.

CASE STUDY 10.1   "As Is"

Prudential Insurance Company of America v. Jefferson Associates, Ltd., 839 SW 2d 866 (Tex. App. 1992). The seller sold an office building that contained asbestos. The buyer brought suit alleging fraud and violations of the Deceptive Trade Practices Act. The court held that an "as is" clause in a contract does not preclude as a matter of law tort actions for fraud and Deceptive Trade Practice violations.

Grube v. Thieol, Ct. App. Wisconsin No. 91-2322, 1992. Wisconsin law imposes a duty on real estate brokers to conduct a reasonably competent, diligent investigation of the property. The court ruled that an "as is" clause in a real estate contract does not necessarily bar negligence and misrepresentation when a real estate broker makes affirmative representations about a property.

What is considered an environmental contaminant? Consider the hazardous material disclosure form that Florida real estate firms give to prospective buyers, as shown in the following box.

Generally, additional information pertaining to these substances is available from the EPA or the state department of Health and Rehabilitative Services.

Sample Hazardous Material Disclosure

There are many hazardous materials that could affect the properties that you may be shown or will inspect as a potential purchaser/renter. The real estate agent will generally have no knowledge of these hazardous materials and does not have the technical expertise to advise you of their presence or to ascertain whether or not they are present.

Hazardous substances in the home may include cleaning chemicals, paint, lawn and garden chemicals, and a variety of indoor air pollutants that can accumulate in improperly ventilated buildings. Hazardous substances outside the home include those found in contaminated land, water, landfills and other disposal sites, and industrial air and water emissions. Some of the more common hazardous substances are asbestos, groundwater contamination, lead-based paint, urea formaldehyde foam insulation, and radon gas.

Adapted from North Broward-Pompano Beach Association of REALTORS® form.

Radon Gas

In the 1990s, disclosure of radon gas to prospective home buyers and tenants became mandatory in many states. The disclosure does not usually require testing of the property prior to closing, but urges the prospective buyer or tenant to complete a radon test (see box below).

Radon Gas Disclosure

Radon gas is a naturally occurring radioactive gas that, when it has accumulated in a building in sufficient quantities, may present health risks to persons who are exposed to it over time. Levels of radon that exceed federal and state guidelines have been found in buildings in this state. You may wish to have a radon test performed at your expense. Additional information regarding radon and radon testing may be obtained from your county public health unit.

Adapted from U.S. Environmental Protection Agency. 1993. *A Citizen's Guide to Radon.* Washington, DC: Public Information Center.

Radon is a colorless, odorless gas that occurs naturally in the earth as a result of the decay of radioactive materials such as uranium. The gas migrates through rocks and soil and is released into the atmosphere and into buildings through their foundations and floors. It attaches itself to dust particles and, as it is breathed in, becomes trapped inside the lungs and attacks their lining. As it continues to decay, it releases small bursts of energy that can damage lung tissue and lead to lung cancer. The result is like exposing a family to hundreds of chest X-rays each year.

The most common way that radon enters homes is through cracks in the foundation and floors or through open areas around drainage pipes, water pumps, or other utilities. Many variables affect the amount of radon in a particular home: the amount of gas emitted, the permeability of the soil, the ease and matter of entry, and the extent to which the house traps it inside. Because of these factors, radon levels may vary significantly from house to house, even within the same neighborhood.

Although a 1996 study cast doubt on the link between radon levels in homes and lung cancer, licensees still are required to disclose radon levels if they are aware of them.

Lead-Based Paint

Lead-based paint has also been a highly publicized environmental contaminant. The EPA estimates lead dust from paint is found in unhealthful concentrations in one of eight U. S. homes. HUD reports that 74 percent of homes built before 1980 contain potentially dangerous levels of the toxin, so there is good reason to recommend inspection.

Typically, lead dust is restricted to isolated spots around the house and scraping and using a lead-dust vacuum will remove it. A city or state health department can suggest a local testing service. HUD requires that all prospective borrowers read and sign a "Lead Paint Poisoning Notification" form at closing if the home was constructed before 1978. Part of this notification form is reproduced in the box on the next page.

In addition to HUD requirements, effective late 1996, sellers and landlords must advise buyers or tenants as well as real estate licensees if the seller/landlord knows about the presence of lead-based paint or paint hazards in the residence. Licensees must make sure that sellers and landlords are aware of their obligations, which include providing written statements and distributing an approved lead hazard information pamphlet.

A $2 million lawsuit brought by first-time home buyers Christian and Melissa Solms illustrates the potential harm of lead-based paint. The Solms sought damages against their real estate agent, mortgage holder, and appraiser and from the Catholic Church, alleging that lead paint in their home caused irreparable brain damage to their baby daughter. The Solms,

Lead Paint Poisoning Notification

The interiors of older homes and apartments often have layers of lead-based paint on the walls, ceilings, window sills, and door frames. Lead-based paint and primers may also have been used on outside porches, railings, garages, fire escapes, and lamp posts. When the paint chips, flakes, or peels off, there may be a real danger for babies and young children.

Children may eat paint chips or chew on painted railings, window sills, or other items when parents are not around. Children can also ingest lead even if they do not specifically eat paint chips. For example, when children play in an area where there are loose paint or dust particles containing lead, they may get these particles on their hands, put their hands into their mouths, and ingest a dangerous amount of lead.

Has your child been especially cranky or irritable? Is your child eating normally? Does your child have stomachaches and vomiting? Does your child complain about headaches? Is your child unwilling to play? These may be signs of lead poisoning, although many times there are no symptoms at all. Lead poisoning can eventually cause mental retardation, blindness, and even death.

If you suspect that your child has eaten chips of paint or someone told you this, you should take your child to the doctor or clinic for testing. If the test shows that your child has an elevated blood lead level, treatment is available. Contact your doctor or local health department for help or more information. Lead screening and treatment are available through the Medicaid Program for those who are eligible.

Adapted from HUD Form "Lead Paint Poisoning Notification." U.S. Environmental Protection Agency, Public Information Center, 401 M Street S.W., Washington, DC 20460.

who purchased the home from the Church, charged that the defendants knowingly withheld information that the 60-year-old former convent had been painted with lead-based paint. The defendants denied the allegation.

The sales agent stated that, after inspecting it themselves, the couple signed a contract agreeing to purchase the home as is. The agent advised the Solms that older homes might have lead-based paint, but the Solms declined to have the home professionally examined. The Solms' attorney argued that the real estate agent should have known that the home had lead paint and that, under Maryland law, she was obligated to warn of the danger. The court eventually ruled in the agent's favor, indicating that she was not responsible for knowing the house contained lead.

Seller Disclosure

Fortunately, most property defects are not likely to result in serious injury or fatalities. Nevertheless, many states have enacted legislation requiring that sellers at the very least acknowledge in writing that they are aware of their duty to disclose latent defects. In other states, sellers must provide a list of any defects of which they are aware. It is likely that over the next few years, state laws will require not only seller disclosure but seller-paid inspections upon request. In anticipation of that day, the prudent real estate practitioner will advise buyers to have a thorough inspection of the property completed before closing. In the interim, the best practice for real estate professionals is to disclose any real or potential environmental or physical defects on the property. Consider the following case studies and how environmental hazards and other physical defects can affect the practice of real estate professionals as well as the buyers and sellers of property.

CASE STUDY 10.2	Environmental Hazards, Physical Defects, and the Real Estate Profession

George v. Lumbrazo, 584, N.Y.S. 2d 704 (App. Div., 1992). The inclusion of an "as is" clause in a contract to sell does not prevent claims for fraud when the sellers covered cracks with paneling to conceal them from the buyers.

A class-action lawsuit has been filed against a developer and real estate brokers for failing to disclose what they knew or should have known about a landfill dump at least a half mile away from a new housing development. According to the lawsuit, the developer and brokers sold homes in the development from 1985 to 1986. Home buyers were not advised that the closed, 57-acre Buzby Landfill was as close as a half-mile from the $100,000-200,000 homes. Buzby is a sanitary landfill, not a hazardous dumpsite and has had no record of health or safety hazards. However, homeowners complained that the proximity of the landfill has jeopardized the resale value of the 200 homes in the development. One of the defendants in the case argued that the court ruling indicates that off-site facts have to be disclosed but did not define a distance of disclosure. This case is still pending. (Adapted from "Brokers in Quandary: What Distance Is Right Distance for Disclosure?" *Agency Law Quarterly, 1995, p. 1+.)*

(continued)

CASE STUDY 10.2 Environmental Hazards, Physical Defects, and the Real Estate Profession Continued.

In a 1990 Washington state case, an appeals court held that a real estate broker could not be held liable for failing to know and disclose that urea-formaldehyde insulation was present inside the walls of a home. Instead, the court found against the seller for failing to advise the broker of its presence. The court indicated that brokers have a duty to take reasonable steps to avoid disseminating false information to the buyer, but the broker cannot guarantee every statement the seller makes. The court ordered the seller to pay attorney fees and costs.
(Brock v. Tarrant, 57 Wash. App. 562, 789 P. 2d 112, 1990.)

Of 600 homes abandoned more than a decade ago in the Love Canal area, 230 have been sold. The Niagara County, New York, houses are near the site of the nation's first full-fledged environmental disaster. Caused by a chemical dumped into the canal bed in the 1940s and 1950s, the toxic hazard forced the government to move homeowners out of the area. Developers are now considering purchasing the homes for renovation and HUD has announced it will insure mortgages on homes in the area. Buyers, however, must sign a disclaimer acknowledging that they are proceeding at their own risk.

Exercise	How Would YOU Respond?

Using the models for ethical decision making suggested in earlier chapters, respond to these situations. Possible responses are provided at the end of the chapter.

1. The sellers have advised me in confidence that they have a roof leak and do not want me to inform prospective buyers.

_____

_____

_____

2. My sellers want to offer their home "as is." They don't want to make any repairs that may be necessary.

_____

_____

_____

3. My buyers don't want to order any inspections. They think the house looks great and don't want to spend hundreds of dollars.

_____

_____

_____

4. What if my buyers don't ask me anything about the condition of the property and I know of several defects—do I have to tell them about the problems if they don't ask?

_____

_____

_____

5. What if the sellers lied about the condition of their home? Am I responsible if I pass along this misinformation? After all, I'm only the agent.

_____

_____

_____

6. Buyers have hired me to locate secluded property. They told me in confidence that they plan to use the property for dumping. They don't want the neighbors to know because the area residents might protest the location of the dump and delay the purchase.

_____

_____

_____

7. My listing is located near an electric utility substation. I have read a little about the potential hazard of electromagnetic fields (EMFs), but the research is inconclusive. Must I reveal information about something that may or may not be a hazard?

_____

_____

_____

Possible Responses

1. The sellers have advised me in confidence that they have a roof leak and do not want me to inform prospective buyers.

First, advise the sellers that you cannot keep this information confidential. If you did, a buyer could sue both of you for failure to disclose a latent defect. However, although the roof problem must be disclosed, they do not have to pay for the repair; who pays is a matter of negotiation.

It is advisable to find out as much as possible about the operating condition and structure of the property. Some real estate offices and many states require the use of a "Seller's Property Disclosure Statement," a checklist of items that the seller completes as part of the listing process. The form may ask such questions as:

1. Does the property have any filled ground? Do you know of any past or present settling or soil movement problems on the property or on adjacent properties?

2. Do you know of any structural additions or alterations to or the installation, alteration, repair, or replacement of significant components of the structure upon the property completed during or prior to your ownership without an appropriate permit?

3. Is the source of your water public or a private well? If a well, when was the last time the water was checked for safety? Are the water supply pipes copper or galvanized?

4. Is the electrical wiring up to code? Are you aware of any damaged or malfunctioning receptacles or switches?

5. Is the house insulated? What type of insulation?

6. What type of heating system? When was it last inspected? Do you have solar heating?

Special checklists may be created for condominiums, which have unique concerns, and for newly constructed residences.

Having your sellers complete and sign these forms will not prevent a lawsuit, but this precautionary measure would provide evidence that you attempted to determine if there were any material defects on the property.

2. *My sellers want to offer their home "as is." They don't want to make any repairs that may be necessary.*

Many states now require that sellers reveal any latent or hidden defects in the home. Listing it "as is" will not remove this ethical and legal obligation. Sellers may refuse to pay for any repairs but still must reveal any condition in the home that would be material to the buyer's purchase. For example, if the sellers know that their roof leaks or that the air conditioner is cooling poorly, they must disclose this information to the buyer. The buyer may then decide whether to buy the home with these problems.

A real estate agent should be concerned when a seller wants to sell the home as is. It may be a red flag that something is wrong with the home. The agent must ask the necessary questions or be ready to face charges of culpable negligence. Courts expect agents who see a red flag to take the time to discover any potential problems.

Advise the sellers that the amount of repairs required of the seller can be limited to a specific amount, such as 2 percent of the purchase price.

3. *My buyers don't want to order any inspections. They think the house looks great and don't want to spend hundreds of dollars.*

Chances are, if the buyers borrow the money to purchase this home, their lender will require a roof and termite report at a minimum. These inspections will cost around $150–200. For a few hundred dollars more, they can have a licensed inspector check the entire premises, including plumbing, electrical, swimming pool, and air conditioning.

Encourage the buyers (even if you work for the sellers) to have the entire property inspected. The inspector can give them professional advice about the construction of the home, information you should never provide because you have no expertise in this area. When the buyer bears this responsibility, it lessens the possibility of a lawsuit against you and the seller for failing to disclose material information.

4. *What if my buyers don't ask me anything about the condition of the property and I know of several defects—do I have to tell them about the problems if they don't ask?*

Yes, even if your buyers don't ask, you must disclose any material information about the property. In many states, this is not only an ethical responsibility, but a legal obligation.

5. *What if the sellers lied about the condition of their home? Am I responsible if I pass along this misinformation? After all, I'm only the agent.*

Being an agent means you are the expert in the relationship between buyers and sellers. Both parties have a right to rely on this expertise. If you question the truthfulness of the sellers' information, you are obligated to investigate. Because you do not want to imply that you do not trust your sellers, simply ask them for copies of receipts and invoices on repairs the sellers claim to have completed. Advise them that they need copies for IRS purposes (to deduct from their sales price to determine their adjusted sales price) and to help the buyers determine the extent of any warranty protection.

If you see anything unusual about the property—for example, major foundation cracks or water stains on the ceiling—you have the duty of affirmative discovery to ask the sellers about these problems. Advise the sellers that they must disclose any problems or risk a lawsuit.

In addition, always encourage the buyers to seek advice from their own experts, even if you represent the sellers. Such advice will alleviate the liability the sellers may have toward repairs. If the buyers' inspector discovers problems the sellers did not disclose, it is better to negotiate this issue before closing rather than face a lawsuit after closing.

Finally, many real estate offices offer warranty programs that the buyer or seller may purchase. These programs guarantee the home's major working components, usually for one year after closing. If a problem occurs, the buyer calls an 800 number and a local repairman takes care of the problem. In some warranty programs, there is a small deductible. These programs are an excellent marketing tool on older homes and will provide the agent with a method to overcome both objections to purchase and liability for problems detected after closing.

6. *Buyers have hired me to locate secluded property. They told me in confidence that they plan to use the property for dumping. They don't want the neighbors to know because the area residents might protest the location of the dump and delay the purchase.*

This could be a problem for the neighbors, your buyers, the sellers, the city, and your broker. You need to verify whether the land is zoned for waste storage, landfill, or dumping. You also need to find out what the buyers intend to dump on the property. If the buyers' purpose is illegal based on zoning or the kind of material being dumped, you should talk to your broker and consider giving up employment with these buyers.

If their objective is legal, you may have another problem with which to wrestle. Some communities have fairly liberal policies regarding the storage of toxic waste or have zoned dumping areas or landfills near residential areas. So even if the use is legal, it may represent a potential hazard to nearby residents.

7. *My listing is located near an electric utility substation. I have read a little about the potential health hazard of electromagnetic fields (EMFs), but the research is inconclusive. Must I reveal information about something that may or may not be a hazard?*

It is true that the research about EMFs is inconclusive. Exposure to EMFs may produce changes in living cells under laboratory conditions, but research hasn't proven whether there may be any harm from these changes.

You may need more data before you decide about disclosure. Look into the location of the substation and the level of EMFs it generates. A prudent course would be to disclose the proximity of the substation to interested buyers and provide them with information about EMFs. Local utility companies can provide you with brochures, or you may write to the Human Health Department, EPA, 401 M Street SW, Washington DC 20460. You may also advise consumers to visit the *New England Journal of Medicine* website at www.nejm.com and the Environmental Protection Agency's website at www.epa.gov/.

Applying Ethics: Working with Colleagues and Employers

You better min' . . . and you better min' who you doin' it to.

American Negro Spiritual

Achieving and maintaining harmony among real estate practitioners can challenge the best of brokers. The real estate business thrives on competition and individual performance. State and federal laws encourage practitioners to obey the spirit and letter of independent contractorship. Thus, it can be difficult to instill a sense of cooperation among real estate professionals, whether the office is large or small. Brokers who strive for teamwork often use a policy manual to define acceptable office performance and behavior. The best manual will not prevent problems; however, it does provide a structure for brokers to act consistently and fairly with all agents.

Unfortunately, authors of policy manuals cannot always anticipate the problems that arise in an office. Even more problematic, one firm's manual may have limited bearing on the behavior of another firm. Because agents from different offices often work together to consummate real estate transactions, their competitive instincts must be subordinated to more cooperative ones. The thousands of complaints filed each year against licensees by licensees at the state and professional level attest to the sad fact that cooperation among brokers and agents often does not happen.

While state statutes often define relationships between real estate agents and their clients, few state or federal statutes mention the ethical obligations agents have to one another.

As discussed in Chapter 6, in its *Code of Ethics,* the NAR also prescribes professional ideals to which members subscribe. A current copy of the *Code of Ethics: National Association of REALTORS®* can be obtained directly from the NAR or by visiting its website at www.realtor.com.

The California and NAR standards provide criteria against which real estate agents can measure their own behavior in working with office colleagues or competitive agents.

EXERCISE

If you were to write a "Ten Commandments" for your real estate office, what would you include? (You may use "Thou shall" and "Thou shall not" language.)

1. _____

2. _____

3. _____

4. _____

5. _____

6. _____

7. _____

8. _____

9. _____

10. _____

EXERCISE

If you were to write a "Ten Commandments" for relationships with agents outside of the office, what would you include? (You may use "Thou shall" and "Thou shall not" language.)

1. _____

2. _____

3. _____

4. _____

5. _____

6. _____

7. _____

8. _____

9. _____

10. _____

Of the many disputes that real estate practitioners have with one another, the most common is procuring cause. Procuring cause issues typically arise when customers (usually buyers) are working with a number of agents who share the same inventory (typically the local MLS). Battles over procuring cause and the resulting wars over commissions can be eliminated by a number of methods:

- Encourage clients and customers to commit to exclusive relationships, preferably in writing. Many states require agency relationships be committed to in writing.
- Educate customers about the shared inventory of local real estate agents, agency relationships, and commission splitting.
- Avoid the appearance of abandoning buyers and sellers. Keep them informed of your activity on their behalf.
- Give buyers business cards and encourage them to hand them to other agents when they are seeking property on their own to identify that they are already working with a broker. Discourage them from seeking property without assistance.
- Ask potential buyers if they are working with another salesperson. If so, ask for a list of properties they have already viewed.

NAR has written extensively about the issue of procuring cause in its *Code of Ethics and Arbitration Manual,* which provides a series of questions to assist practitioners as well as hearing panels in carefully analyzing the conduct of the parties.

Another common problem among real estate practitioners happens when agents fail to respect exclusivity. When clients identify an agent as their exclusive representative, all other agents should contact that representative directly. Only in rare circumstances should an agent contact the principal directly.

The submission of offers, particularly multiple offers, is also a potential problem. Again, if sellers have identified an exclusive agent, all offers must be submitted through that agent. Real estate practitioners also have an ethical obligation to present all offers—regardless of price, terms, or format—as quickly as possible. You must communicate even the possibility of offers to the principal.

To obtain the most favorable terms for the client, real estate practitioners should cooperate with all salespersons, unless cooperating would somehow harm the client. The possibility of earning a higher commission by refusing to present a competitor's offer or to allow a competitor to show the property should not be a consideration.

You should not criticize your competitor's business or business practices unless you can do so in an objective, professional manner. If asked about a competitor, avoid negative comments such as, "Sailaway Realty is a terrible company—their sales staff is inexperienced." Instead, comment positively and deflect attention back to your office: "Sailaway Realty is a good company. But let me tell you why my firm could do a better job marketing your property."

Harass Thy Competitor

Real estate brokers often harass alternative competitors, a practice that costs home buyers and sellers money, claims the Consumer Federation of America. The study showed that while discrimination had declined since the 1970s, it was still fairly common. Of the 85 discounters and buyer brokers polled, 60 percent reported disparagement of their business by regular brokers, 35 percent reported pirating of their clients by regular brokers, and 30 percent reported that regular brokers refused to show homes listed by alternative brokers. The 17-city survey showed that consumers who did not use buyer brokers pay up to five percent more for a house. Consumers who do not use discount brokers pay commissions between one to three percentage points higher than what discounters charge.

Adapted from the *Palm Beach Post*, 12 September 1993.

Treating firms differently because of their relationship to the principal, and offering unequal commission splits, may also be perceived as unethical. Consider the following case study on price fixing.

| CASE STUDY 11.1 | A Twist on Price-Fixing |

Smythe, Cramer Co. of Cleveland, one of the largest independent brokerage firms in the U.S., was charged with maintaining a discriminatory policy against buyer brokers. The $75 million lawsuit was filed by Stephen and Kathleen Jacobs on behalf of an estimated 500 home buyers who, they said, paid higher prices because of the firm's policies. The lawsuit claimed that listing agents for Smythe, Cramer offered buyer brokers only a 20 percent commission split while traditional seller brokers received more equitable treatment. The Jacobs argued they were forced to pay a higher price for their home because the company would not cooperate with their brokers. They also maintained that home sellers suffered because prospects may have been steered away from their properties since buyer agents were uncertain of their compensation.

Symthe, Cramer contended that the courts cannot fix commission splits between cooperating brokers due to federal price-fixing regulations. While awaiting the court's decision the firm ended the policy of offering smaller splits to buyer brokers. The trial court dismissed the case, and the appellate court affirmed its dismissal.

Withholding information about a property from a cooperative colleague can create additional ethical concerns. Consider the case study on the following page.

Certain business practices in real estate have been characterized as unfair: asking an owner when a listing will expire, claiming to be a specialist when no special training or experience warrants such a claim, giving the impression that a firm has sold a property when in fact it has not, allowing a transaction to fail because of a commission dispute, and failing to give information on a listing promptly.

The relationship between brokers and their sales staff is also fraught with ethical concerns. In most states, brokers are liable for the actions of their agents, so it behooves brokers to supervise their salespeople closely. Similarly, salespeople are obligated to follow office policies and their broker's directives and to keep office matters confidential.

In addition to brokers' legal responsibilities, they also have ethical obligations to their salespeople. For example, ethical hiring practices would include being truthful about income potential, providing appropriate training, avoiding discrimination, encouraging continuing education, and providing written policies regarding commission splits. Brokers also should develop fair and equitable procedures for handling disputes and terminating unproductive agents.

Code of Ethics Enforcement

In 1998, the National Association of REALTORS® (NAR) established a Presidential Advisory Group (PAG) on Code of Ethics Enforcement. The PAG was asked to determine how the Code is enforced; to develop strategies to help local associations understand their role in Code enforcement and act on complaints; and to increase awareness of ethics.

The PAG made 16 recommendations addressing ethics issues and what NAR should do. Among the 16 recommendations:

- Make ethics orientation mandatory for all members.
- Set standard national guidelines for imposing discipline for Code of Ethics violations.
- Make it a required membership duty to report potential Code violations.
- Develop alternative enforcement procedures, including trained hearing officers, mediation, and ombudsman.

The Code of Ethics can be found at NAR's website at www.nar.realtor. com. The PAG's complete and final report can be found at www.realtor.com.

Source: Maryann Bassett, CRB, CRS, member of NAR's PAG on Code of Ethics Enforcement, private correspondence.

State laws often govern the payment of broker commissions to their agents and require that salespersons cannot receive payment from anyone except their brokers. By the same token, brokers have an ethical responsibility to pay their agents promptly and fairly.

In most states, business generated by a salesperson "belongs" to the broker. That is, any listings, sales, or leads are the broker's property. If the relationship between the broker and salesperson is terminated, current, pending, and future transactions originated in that office remain with the broker. To take business away from an employing broker is a breach of trust and, in some cases, larceny.

Real estate brokers and agents also have an ethical and professional responsibility to keep up-to-date on practices, principles, and the law. In fact, most states require continuing education to maintain licensure. However, these requirements establish a legal minimum in terms of professional education and often can be satisfied with a correspondence course. A professional real estate agent should seek regular and extensive training beyond the state-required minimum.

A good case can be made for the ethical obligation of agents to share information with other licensees in order to protect the public. Do real estate

| CASE STUDY 11.2 | Commission Feud |

R eal estate agents who handled the $7.3 million sale of Florida ocean-
front property are battling over the $400,000 commission from the
transaction. The selling salesperson claims that her broker fired her
before the sale closed and denied her her share of the commission, esti-
mated at over $100,000. The broker said the salesperson was dismissed
from the firm because of differences in business philosophy.

*Adapted from Linus Chua, "Real Estate Agents Feud Over Commission," Palm Beach
Post, 13 April 1995, p. 17A.*

Exercise

How could this dispute have been avoided?

_____

_____

How should this dispute be resolved?

_____

_____

Getting By

Texas requires brokers to complete 15 hours of continuing education
every two years. When the law came up for renewal in 1991, a legislator
added a provision that gave a lifetime exemption to brokers who paid a
$7 fee, had 10 or more years of experience, operated in a county with
225,000 or fewer people (254 of Texas' 263 counties fit this description),
and filed their paperwork during a 30-day period.

Nearly one in four Texas brokers bypassed the state's continuing education requirements in this way. The legislator who proposed the provision
is a licensed real estate broker.

*Adapted from National Association of REALTORS®. May 1992. "A Loser's List." Real
Estate Today.*

practitioners have a similar ethical obligation to report to the appropriate authorities those agents who fail to keep current or who withhold vital information? Professional real estate agents might argue that incompetent agents implicate all agents, so agents who ignore their professional obligation and fail to keep current pose a hazard to the profession as well as the public and should be barred from practicing real estate.

State regulatory agencies rarely entertain disputes over unethical conduct of a licensee. The regulators' mission is to protect the public from dishonest licensees, not the licensee from other licensees. What recourse does the practitioner have when the dispute is a matter of ethics, not legalities? Members of a local association of REALTORS® may air their grievances in front of a committee of their peers. A decision against a member could result in anything from a reprimand to expulsion from the organization. Other alternatives are mediation, binding arbitration, or litigation.

Exercise	How Would YOU Respond?

Using the models for ethical decision making suggested in earlier chapters, respond to these questions. Possible responses are provided at the end of the chapter.

1. I have spent a lot of time working with a couple. I finally showed them a home they liked enough to submit an offer. As I finished filling out the offer forms, the wife stated that they had seen the home before with another real estate salesperson the weekend before I met them. What should I do?

_____

_____

_____

_____

2. I had a good offer on a property listed by a competitor. When I called the broker to make an appointment to present the offer, the broker advised me that the property was under contract already and due to close in a month. The broker refused to present my offer. Was the broker right?

_____

_____

_____

_____

3. I told a competing broker that my sellers were going to submit an offer in two days on property that broker had listed. The broker called me back in the interim and advised me that he found a buyer whose offer was accepted. Shouldn't the broker have advised his sellers that another offer was pending?

_____

_____

_____

_____

4. I am thinking about leaving my broker for a firm that offers greater financial and business opportunities. What do I need to do?

_____

_____

_____

_____

5. My broker asked me to do something I believe is unethical. What should I do?

_____

_____

_____

_____

6. A cooperating agent from a neighboring community used her forms to present an offer. I was unfamiliar with those forms and told her so before we made the presentation together. She failed to reveal that her contract called for the seller to pay for certain closing costs that my contract required the buyer to pay. Wasn't she obligated to tell me and the client about those differences?

_____

_____

_____

_____

Possible Responses

1. I have spent a lot of time working with a couple. I finally showed them a home they liked enough to submit an offer. As I finished filling out the offer forms, the wife stated that they had seen the home before with another real estate salesperson the weekend before I met them. What should I do?

Find out why the buyers did not submit an offer through the first salesperson. It is possible that your sales skills demonstrated that the property was affordable or your diligent work proved to them that this was the best of the available properties. The first salesperson may have offended the buyers in some way so that they did not want to continue working with that salesperson or firm. In any of these cases, you should talk with your broker about your ethical responsibility to the first salesperson. If you determine that you are the procuring cause, you legally owe nothing to the other salesperson. You may, on the other hand, wish to offer some kind of compensation for the other salesperson's efforts. You can eliminate this procuring cause problem by asking buyers what properties they have already previewed with other salespersons.

2. I had a good offer on a property listed by a competitor. When I called the broker to make an appointment to present the offer, the broker advised me that the property was under contract already and due to close in a month. The broker refused to present my offer. Was the broker right?

No. The broker must submit all offers as long as the property sale has not closed. The seller decides whether to consider other offers during a pending transaction. If the seller doesn't want any other offers submitted, the broker should request that in writing so that such problems are addressed.

The broker should submit all offers for a practical reason as well: the seller can accept the second offer as a backup contract. Then, if the initial contract falls apart, the broker can still have a viable sale.

You should discuss a listing broker's refusal to present your offer with your broker and other advisors, such as local association members. Your broker should contact the listing broker, and, if unsuccessful in getting your offer presented, consider filing a grievance with your association.

3. I told a competing broker that my sellers were going to submit an offer in two days on property that broker had listed. The broker called me back in the interim and advised me that he found a buyer whose offer was accepted. Shouldn't the broker have advised his sellers that another offer was pending?

Yes. In fairness to the agent's client, not only should the listing broker's offer be submitted, but the possibility of other incoming offers should also be revealed. It is possible that the listing broker concealed the possibility of your offer from a concern that if a cooperating agent were involved, the listing broker's commission would be significantly reduced.

While handling multiple offers can be nerve-wracking, a seller should be advised to evaluate all offers and counter all viable offers with a request that the buyers make their best offer within a specified time period. That way, the seller can choose the best among them. (In some areas, only one offer is presented at a time, although the seller is informed of all possible offers.)

Considerations about the size of the broker's commission should always be secondary to the best interests of the client. To do otherwise is an ethical breach and, in some states, a violation of statutes.

4. *I am thinking about leaving my broker for a firm that offers greater financial and business opportunities. What do I need to do?*

There are a number of legal, ethical, and procedural matters to consider as you terminate your relationship with your broker. Before giving notice, review the policy manual regarding the firm's termination procedures. The manual usually addresses issues such as the disbursement of commissions on pending sales, returning proprietary items such as office keys and signs, and notifying clients regarding the management of their accounts.

While many brokers pay a commission on pending transactions as long as the salesperson continues to follow up on the details leading to a closing, state laws usually do not require a broker to do so. It's advisable, then, if your broker does not have a written policy regarding commissions on pending transactions, to discuss this issue when you give notice.

You may wish to give your broker a list of your current and pending transactions, detailing what you have taken care of so far and what remains to be done and recommending a salesperson to take over the business with your customers and clients.

It is unethical to contact your customers and clients after you leave your broker, as you could be diverting your broker's business. You may contact them only with the permission of your broker and with utmost tact and discretion. You might say, "Ms. Brown, I'm calling to let you know that I am no longer affiliated with Super Realty as of this coming week. However, the company will still be handling your property and has assigned Salesperson Smith to continue the broker's fine work. May Salesperson Smith meet with you this week to review the marketing of your property and to get to know you?"

Most customers and clients will want to follow you to your next employer. After all, they have established a relationship with you and haven't even met your broker. That is why your employer will probably prefer to handle the transfer of your business themselves. Any questions your clients have about your new business relationship should be deferred to your present employer. If your clients wish to follow you, disclose to them and to your new broker any ethical conflicts you have in maintaining your relationship with them.

Plan to give the firm at least one week's notice so that the broker can adjust the floor duty and advertising schedules. If you are an independent contractor, you can, of course, terminate your relationship on a moment's notice, but you will appear unprofessional.

You may want to give written notice to the broker in person. Be prepared for the broker to give you an exit interview. If concerned about staff and company, the broker will want to know why you are leaving and may even want to negotiate with you, offering terms that are competitive with those of your new employer.

After you leave, you may not discuss proprietary information with your new employer. You enjoyed a fiduciary relationship with your past broker—a relationship of trust and confidence. Any confidential information must remain so forever. It would also be unethical for you to disparage your previous employer to anyone. Return any of the broker's property before leaving: client files, office and property keys, books, and manuals. Do not remove or photocopy any files. Promptly notify your local board and state real estate commission of your change of employer and address.

5. *My broker asked me to do something I believe is unethical. What should I do?*

Discuss the problem with trusted friends and advisors and then approach your broker with your concerns. (Remember, you cannot share client confidences.) If you continue to feel that you are being asked to do something unethical, you may want to terminate your employment with that broker. (Brokers who think an agent's conduct is unethical should also consider terminating the employment.)

6. *A cooperating agent from a neighboring community used her forms to present an offer. I was unfamiliar with those forms and told her so before we made the presentation together. She failed to reveal that her contract called for the seller to pay for certain closing costs that my contract required the buyer to pay. Wasn't she obligated to tell me and the client about those differences?*

The cooperating agent had a responsibility to the seller to be honest about all the terms of the contract. If aware of the significant differences between contracts, she should have revealed them to you. However, you also had a duty to be familiar with the terms of the contract because of your fiduciary relationship with the seller. When you work with cooperating agents, you cannot transfer your burden of responsibility to them. The responsibilities should be shared. Consult with an attorney if you are using an unfamiliar contract form.

Applying Ethics: Community and Public Concerns

Men of integrity, by their very existence, rekindle the belief that as a people, we can live above the level of moral squalor.

John Gardner

Real estate agents have influential roles in the community. Among other concerns, they preserve neighborhood values, lobby for favorable real estate tax legislation, oppose detrimental land use, control growth, and support planning. Responding unethically to these challenges risks irreparable harm to the community and injures the credibility of all real estate agents in that community.

Brokers should treat members of the public fairly, not only with respect to race, religion, color, national origin, gender, handicap, and family status, but also with respect to other differences. For example, the Fair Housing Act does not refer to marital status as a protected class; nevertheless, real estate practitioners should treat single, married, divorced, and separated people equally. Brokers should respect cultural differences among their clients and customers; learning a second language or taking courses on working with an international clientele may be helpful.

Brokers and agents must take every precaution to handle client and customer money carefully. Most states require that anything of value turned over to a licensee be placed into an escrow account promptly. Disputes over escrow funds should be handled in accordance with the law and with respect to the concerns of the parties.

CASE STUDY 12.1   Opportunity Knocking?

Real estate agent David Hartger of Grand Rapids, Michigan, thought that a violent death in a neighborhood was the sound of opportunity knocking.

Hartger wrote a letter to 100 residents of the neighborhood where the fatal shooting occurred, offering to help them sell their homes. His letter read: "With the recent increase of violence in the neighborhood and fears of street gangs in the area, many homeowners are wondering if it is safe to raise a family, or even own a home, in your neighborhood." The letter offended the residents, and the Grand Rapids Association of REALTORS® is investigating the case. In the meantime, Hartger's employer apologized for his bad judgment. Hartger later said, "My intentions weren't to do any harm. My intention to promote myself was at a bad time and a bad decision, and the wording of it was bad, too."

Adapted from *Palm Beach Post*, 31 May 1993, p. 3.

One way that real estate agents reach consumers is advertising. Practitioners should ensure that their advertising complies with state laws and does not deceive or misrepresent. For example, properties that have closed or are off the market should not be advertised to generate leads.

Agents who want to purchase property themselves should make it clear to the sellers early on that they are real estate experts to level the playing field and give the sellers opportunity to obtain assistance and representation, if necessary. Agents who act as sellers should also disclose as soon as possible that they have special knowledge that could place prospective buyers at a disadvantage.

Real estate practitioners have a responsibility to advise clients and customers of any limitation in their expertise. For example, agents who are asked to handle the sale of a business but have no experience in business brokerage should advise the client of their limited expertise.

Clients and customers often ask practitioners about services related to the real estate transaction, such as title work, surveying, appraisal, and inspection. It is best to provide a list of competent professionals who provide those services rather than to recommend a single individual. Accepting rebates or gifts from these referrals is unethical and may violate RESPA as well. The buyer often pays for these referral fees or gifts in increased costs.

Licensees should keep current on legislative or political matters that influence housing, zoning, and land use. They are obligated to use their knowledge and influence to shape changes that will benefit the public. Members of NAR, for example, contribute to a political action committee to ensure that their sentiments are heard in Congress. At a local level, agents often contribute to politicians who favor specific real estate legislation.

Consider the ethical issues in the following case study.

Considering Campaign Contributions

Plymouth developer Robert DeMattia contributed $2,500 in 1992 to the campaign fund of County Executive Edward McNamara and $2,000 to the campaign coffers of Arthur Blackwell, chairman of the Wayne County Board of Commissioners and recently announced mayoral candidate in Detroit. In addition, DeMattia last year made small contributions of about $100 to 9 of the 14 other county commissioners.

DeMattia appears to be the county's choice to develop a 700-acre parcel of county land in Northville Township (Michigan). The county executive's office has made the DeMattia group its front-runner to develop the site for mixed residential and commercial use from among three other teams that bid on the property. When a selection is made, the executive's office will send the nomination to the 15-member Board of Commissioners for approval.

Some members of the other three teams competing for the Northville Township land made small contributions to McNamara's campaign chest last year. Alan Kiriluk, president of Kirco Realty & Development Ltd., individually made a $250 contribution to McNamara's fund, according to county campaign-finance records. Kirco is competing to manage the development in Northville Township. Robert Halso, president of Pulte Homes of Michigan in Royal Oak, individually contributed $1,000 to McNamara's campaign last year. Pulte also seeks to manage the project.

Blackwell said he will vote on the county executive's recommended selection based on the merits of the bid, not on any campaign contributions. He said he never would oppose a selection just because a group of developers did not contribute to his campaign. DeMattia said campaign contributions are of little influence. He contributes to political campaigns because business leaders should take a responsibility in ensuring good government, he adds. The contributions, he said, are his method of participating fully in the political process rather than actively campaigning for candidates.

Adapted from D. Barkholz, 1993. "Property Bidders also Active Campaign Donors." *Crain's Detroit Business.* © 1993 Crain Communications.

Real estate practitioners have a civic responsibility to participate in the democratic process; however, they also have an obligation to the public to make their political contributions with the community's interest first and their own interest second.

In addition, real estate professionals have a responsibility to the public to continue their education beyond the state-required minimum coursework, as discussed in Chapter Eleven. Finally, licensees should support state regulatory measures that work toward enhancing the professionalism of all real estate agents.

CASE STUDY 12.2   Virtual Violations

Two Ohio real estate agents became the first licensees to be found guilty of fraud and negligence because of their websites. The Ohio Real Estate Commission found that among other violations, the licensees had failed to disclose their firm affiliation on every page of their website. Real estate professionals must make sure that on all forms of communication, including webpages and e-mail, that their status as licensees and office affiliation are clear. Listing information that is posted electronically must also be updated frequently. Spamming, copyright infringement, and unlicensed activity are other issues that state regulators are investigating.

From "Virtual Violations," by Michael J. Russer, *Real Estate Technology,* 1998–99, pp. 20–22.

Exercise   How Would YOU Respond?

Using the models for ethical decision making suggested in earlier chapters, respond to these questions. Possible responses are provided at the end of the chapter.

1. I am a licensee in a medium-sized brokerage firm. I have witnessed several instances where my broker's checks have bounced. I don't have access to the books, but I gather from the secretary that some of my escrow checks are being deposited in the broker's general operating account instead of into the trust account. Sometimes my closings have been postponed for no apparent reason and then we were coincidentally able to close when a new sale was made and another deposit was received. I suspect my broker is embezzling funds. What should I do?

2. Our firm had a new listing in a very good location at a reasonable price. When we advertised, we received a heavy response and sold the home the first evening we showed it. We would like to generate more business for our other listings. Is there any harm in continuing to advertise the home that has already sold?

3. A firm in our community advertises that it will give a free microwave oven with every home purchased during this month. Is this practice fair and ethical?

4. I am an active licensee who wishes to sell my own property. Must I list it through my brokerage? If not, when I advertise, must I place a notice in the advertisement that I am a licensee?

5. Even though the Kennedy family described its ocean-front home as having "run-of-the-mill" architecture, its sales brochure claimed the residence as "one of the most historically significant private residences" and "an exceptionally fine example of the work of [architect Addison] Mizner." The broker who wrote the description explained, "You have to understand, my job is to sell ice to the Eskimos, and I happen to be one of the best at it. . . . We took that liberty, a creative liberty. It was certainly an angle we wanted to exploit." (From "Ads Can Be Used Against You." Palm Beach Post, April 21, 1995, p. 2B.) What is the difference between taking "a creative liberty" and misrepresenting a property's features?

Possible Responses

1. *I am a licensee in a medium-sized brokerage firm. I have witnessed several instances where my broker's checks have bounced. I don't have access to the books, but I gather from the secretary that some of my escrow checks are being deposited in the broker's general operating account instead of into the trust account. Sometimes my closings have been postponed for no apparent reason and then we were coincidentally able to close when a new sale was made and another deposit was received. I suspect my broker is embezzling funds. What should I do?*

   Before you make any accusations, obtain as much information as possible about the management of your broker's escrow funds. Then talk to your broker. If you find evidence that your suspicions are true, contact your personal attorney and, depending on your attorney's advice, notify the state regulatory agency. (Many regulatory agencies allow you to report such problems anonymously.) You should also consider terminating your relationship with your broker.

2. *Our firm had a new listing in a very good location at a reasonable price. When we advertised, we received a heavy response and sold the home the first evening we showed it. We would like to generate more business for our other listings. Is there any harm in continuing to advertise the home that has already sold?*

   Consider how the sellers of that home would feel about your firm's use of their property to generate leads. If they don't mind the continued advertising, you may want to have a letter from them to that effect. Consider the buyer's feelings as well. Equally important, consider the public. How will potential buyers feel if you indicate that the house is for sale when it is not? You might want to try advertising the property as "pending—will consider back-up offers" (if that is the case) and encourage prospects to look at your other listings as well.

3. *A firm in our community advertises that it will give a free microwave oven with every home purchased during this month. Is this practice fair and ethical?*

   In some states, it is acceptable to share commission with a principal as a gift. (Referral fees to a nonprincipal, however, are unlawful.) However, offering an inducement to purchase, including the offering of an appraisal in any advertising or promotional material, is illegal. Your state regulatory commission needs to decide whether your competitor is breaking the law. If your competitor is not breaking the law, but you feel the ad poses an unfair advantage, you may want to talk with your competitor or consider making a similar offer to principals to eliminate the advantage.

4. *I am an active licensee who wishes to sell my own property. Must I list it through my brokerage? If not, when I advertise, must I place a notice in the advertisement that I am a licensee?*

Your broker may have a policy regarding agents selling their own property or may have an incentive for agents who list property through the firm. Although no state law mandates that you must list your property through your broker, you should notify your employer as a courtesy and to avoid possible conflict.

If you advertise the property on your own, state law or professional standards (such as NAR rules) may dictate what the ad states about your licensing status. If your state or professional society has no particular demands on your advertising, you may want to indicate that you are an "owner-agent" so that other licensees do not waste time trying to get your listing.

At the very least, you should advise interested buyers of your expertise when they express a serious interest in the property. Many states require that whether you are active or inactive, if you are a principal you must notify the other party (preferably in writing) that you have license status. Again, notification may not have to be in the advertisement, but it should be no later than at the time of offer.

5. *What is the difference between taking "a creative liberty" and misrepresenting a property's features?*

Many states have statutes governing deceptive trade practices. Exaggerating a product's qualities or attributes could be a deceptive practice. In real estate, the difference between "puffing" a property's qualities and misrepresenting them could depend on whether the buyers can 1) examine the property on their own; 2) verify the information independently; or 3) rely exclusively on the practitioner's expertise. While it may be appropriate to say, "Isn't this living room the most spacious you've ever seen?" it would be ethically inappropriate to say the living room is 15' × 20' when, in fact, it's 10' × 10'. Although the broker claims "creative liberty," if the home is not significant architecturally, in the opinion of experts, then the broker should omit his statement from the ad.

A Closing Note

Ethical dilemmas are not the private property of real estate practitioners, but in fact are inherent in many situations. This is obvious every time we read or watch the news. Public personalities from the fields of medicine, politics, sports, and entertainment confront ethical dilemmas before the nation and the world. Perhaps some of these dilemmas appear more dramatic and threatening than those confronting real estate professionals; nevertheless, moral issues are increasing in frequency and complexity.

Our complicated society asks each of us to play many roles. Gender differences and diverse religious beliefs sometimes spark conflicts of interest, hidden agendas, improprieties, and perceptual problems. Multicultural communities and workplaces may heighten the sense of differences among us and create conflicts between values and goals.

In addition to conflicts born of our increasingly complex society, each of us carries enormous responsibilities. As real estate practitioners, we are the gatekeepers of the American dream of home ownership; we are guardians for appropriate land use and a clean environment; we provide invaluable service to businesses, citizens, and government; and the results of our work fuel the economy. Although wrestling with ethical dilemmas is not an everyday experience, ethical dilemmas are becoming more commonplace. We read more and more often about moral failures, individual and institutional. As technological, demographic, and social changes push us into the next century, our talents and skills will stretch to their limits. The ultimate challenge to confront us—as real estate professionals and human beings—will be to do the right thing.

Appendix: Resources for More Information on Ethics

Organizations

Boston University Center for
Advancement of Ethics and Character
Education
www.education.bu.eus/CharacterEd

Ethics Resource Center
600 New Hampshire NW, Suite 400
Washington, DC 20037
www.ethics.org

Josephson Institute for the
Advancement of Ethics
4640 Admiralty Way
Marina Del Rey, CA 90292
www.josephsoninstitute.org

Center for the Study of Ethical
Development
206 A Burton Hall
University of Minnesota
178 Pillsbury Drive
Minneapolis, MN 55455

Minnesota Center for Corporate
Responsibility
1000 La Salle Avenue
Minneapolis, MN 55403
www.tigger.stthomas.edu/mccr/

Publications of Interest

Journals and Newsletters

Agency Law Quarterly. Box 3422,
Arlington, VA 22203.

**Ethics Resource Center's newsletter
(and other educational material).*
600 New Hampshire NW, Suite
400, Washington, DC 20037

Insights on Global Ethics. Institute for
Global Ethics, Box 563, Camden,
ME 04843, www.globalethics.org.

*Penn, W.Y. (May, 1990). Teaching
ethics: A direct approach. *Journal
of Moral Education, 2,* 124–138.

Pike, L. B. (1985). Values and moral
education for the adult throughout
the life span: An annotated bibliog-
raphy. ERIC document
#ED260182.

Today's REALTOR®. National Association of REALTORS®, 430 North
Michigan Avenue, Chicago, IL
60611, www.nar.realtor.com.

Books

*Blanchard, K. and Peale, N.V. (1989). *The power of ethical management.* New York: Fawcett.

*Covey, S. (1989). *The seven habits of highly effective people.* New York: Simon & Schuster.

*Covey, S. (1990). *Principle-centered leadership.* NY: Simon & Schuster.

DeMars, Nan (1997). *You Want Me to Do What?* New York: Fireside Books.

Dosick, Wayne (1993). *The business bible: Ten new commandments for creating an ethical workplace.* New York: HarperBusiness.

Driscoll, Dawn; Hoffman, Michael; and Petry, Edward (1995). *The Ethical Edge.* New York: Mastermedia.

Gilligan, Carol (1982). *In a different voice: Psychological theory and women's development.* Cambridge, Massachusetts: Harvard University Press.

Hunt, Morton (1990). *The compassionate beast: What science is discovering about the humane side of humankind.* New York: William Morrow and Co.

Josephson, Michael, and Hanson, Wes (1998). *Power of Character.* San Francisco: Jossey-Bass.

Kidder, Rushworth M. (1995). *How good people make tough choices: Resolving the dilemmas of ethical living.* New York: William Morrow and Company.

Kidder, Rushworth M. (1994). *Shared values for a troubled world: Conversations with men and women of conscience.* San Francisco: Jossey-Bass.

Lewis, H. (1990). *A question of values: Six ways we make the personal choices that shape our lives.* San Francisco: HarperCollins.

*Lickona, T. (1992). *Educating for character.* New York: Bantam Books.

Lyons, G., Harlan, D., and Reilly, J. (1993). *Consensual dual agency.* Chicago: Real Estate Education Company.

Pivar, W. H., and Harlan, D. L. (1995). *Real estate ethics* (3rd ed.). Chicago: Real Estate Education Company.

Reilly, J. W. (1994). *Agency relationships in real estate 4th edition.* Chicago: Real Estate Education Company.

Runner, E. J. (1992). *Ethics: Its impact on real estate.* New York: Vantage Press.

*Rest, J. (1987). *Moral judgement: An interesting variable for higher education research.* Paper for the annual convention of the Association for the Study of Higher Education, Baltimore, Maryland.

Rest, J. & Narvaez, D. (1994). *Moral development in the professions.* Hillsdale, New Jersey: Lawrence Erlbaum.

Stock, Gregory (1991). *The book of questions: Business, politics and ethics.* New York, NY: Workman Publishing.

Thiroux, J. (1990). *Ethics: Theory and practice.* New York: Macmillan Publishing Company.

Unell, Barbara C. and Wyckoff, Jerry L. (1995). *20 teachable virtues: Practical ways to pass on lessons of virtue and character to your children.* New York: Perigee Books.

*If you have limited time, these resources would provide the most significant reading.

References

ALQ update. (1992). *Agency Law Quarterly, 3,* 92.

Aspen Declaration. (1995). Marina Del Rey, CA: Josephson Institute of Ethics.

Association of Real Estate License Law Officials. (1999). *1998 digest of real estate license laws: U. S. and Canada.* Centerville, UT: Author.

Aydt, Bruce. "I've Got A Secret—Do I Tell?" (1999, May) *Realtor,* p. 50.

Barkholz, D. (1993, August). "Property bidders also active campaign donors." *Crain's Detroit Business, 9,* 31.

Beauchamp, T. L., & Bowie, N. E. (1988). *Ethical theory and business.* Englewood Cliffs, NJ: Prentice-Hall.

Behrman, J. N. (1988). *Essays on ethics in business and the profession.* Englewood Cliffs, NJ: Prentice-Hall.

Benson, G. C. S. (1982). *Business ethics in America.* New York: D. C. Heath and Company.

"Blacks get fewer mortgages than whites." *Palm Beach Post.* January 21, 1995, p. 4B.

"Brokers in Quandary: What distance is right distance for disclosure?" *Agency Law Quarterly,* 1995, p. 17.

"Business majors cheat." *Palm Beach Post.* (1993, September 27), p. 3. [Reprinted from *Ethics Journal,* Ethics Resource Center.]

Carter, F. (1987). *The education of little tree.* Albuquerque: University of New Mexico Press.

Clark, C. (1991, May). *Address for twelfth annual conference of the Real Estate Educators Association.* Paper presented at the 12th annual conference of the Real Estate Educators Association, Orlando, Florida.

Covey, S. (1989). *The seven habits of highly effective people.* New York: Simon and Schuster.

Disclosure of stigmas. (1991, May 13). *Realtor News,* p. 6.

Donaldson, T. (1984). *Case studies in business ethics.* Englewood Cliffs, NJ: Prentice-Hall.

Elam, S. M., Rose, L. C., & Gallup, A. M. (1993, October). The 25th annual PDK Gallup Poll. *Phi Delta Kappan,* pp. 137–152.

Guy, M. E. (1990). *Ethical decision making in everyday work situations.* New York: Quorum Books.

Harris-Bowlsbey, J., Spivack, J. D., & Lisansky, R. S. (1986). *Take hold of your future: Leader's manual.* Towson, MD: ACT Career Planning Services.

Hitt, W. D. (1990). *Ethics and leadership: Putting theory into practice.* Columbus, OH: Batelle Press.

Hoffman, C. (1993, September). "Don't be blind to the buyer's source of money." *Real Estate Today,* p. 10.

Hoffman, W. M. (1989). "The cost of a corporate conscience." *Business and Society Review, 69,* 46–50.

Irwin, D. M. (1982). Moral development. In *Encyclopedia of educational research* (pp. 1237–1240). New York: American Educational Research Association.

Jefferson, J. "Confessed Bank Robber Says Desperation Drove Him to Commit Crime." *Savannah Morning News.* December 5, 1994, p. 5C.

Jones, D. G. (1982). *Doing ethics in business.* Cambridge, MA: Oelgeschlager, Gunn, and Hain.

Kohlberg, L. (1981). *The meaning and measurement of moral development.* Worcester, MA: Clark University Press.

"Legal Briefs," *Realtor News.* Sept. 26, 1994, p. 4.

Lickona, T. (1976). *Moral development and behavior: Theory, research, and social issues.* New York: Holt, Rinehart & Winston.

Lickona, T. (1983). *Raising good children.* New York: Bantam Books.

Lickona, T. (1992). *Educating for character.* New York: Bantam Books.

Long, D. (1990). *What do I say now? A real estate agent's guide to answering tough customer questions.* Chapel Hill, NC: Winter Harbor Enterprises.

A loser's list. (1992, May). *Real Estate Today,* p. 10.

Murray, J. (1993, August 23). "The right way and the strong way." *Palm Beach Post,* p. 8A.

National Fair Housing Advocate, Vol. 5, No. 3, April, 1995.

Nelson, D. R., & Obremski, T. E. (1990). "Promoting moral growth through intra-group participation." *Journal of Business Ethics, 9,* 731–739.

Nicgorski, W. (1987). *An almost chosen people: The moral aspirations of Americans.* Notre Dame: Univ. of Notre Dame Press, 1976.

Randall, D. M., & Gibson, A. M. (1990). "Methodology in business ethics research: A review and critical assessment." *Journal of Business Ethics, 9,* 457–471.

Russer, Michael (1998–99). "Virtual violations." *Real Estate Technology,* pp. 20–24.

Thiroux, J. (1990). *Ethics: Theory and practice.* New York: Macmillan Publishing Company.

Trevino, L. K. (1992). "Moral reasoning and business ethics: Implications for research, education, and management." *Journal of Business Ethics, 11,* 445–459.

U.S. Environmental Protection Agency. (1993). *A citizen's guide to radon.* Washington, DC: Public Information Center.

"White couple to sell home to settle racial bias law suit," *Palm Beach Post,* January 3, 1994, p. 29A.

Index

Advertising, 124, 128
AIDS, 93, 95–96, 97–98
Agency and non-agency relationships,
    63–76
   buyer brokerage, 64, 65, 66
   dual agency brokerage, 64, 65
   Edina Realty, 65
   facilitation, 65
   mediation, 65
   seller brokerage, 63
   single agency brokerage, 64
   sub-agency, 63
   transaction brokerage, 65
ARELLO, 2
"As is," 100
Aspen Declaration, 24

Bentham, Jeremy, 27, 28
Buber, Martin, 28, 35
Buyer brokerage, 64, 65, 66

Campaign contributions, 125
Cheating, 13
Child molester, 46
Civil rights, 77–91
   and the broker, 79
   and the developer, 80
   of the disabled, 78
   of home buyers, 77
Civil Rights Act of 1866, 77

Civil Rights Act of 1968, 77, 86
   condominiums, 86
   exemptions, 86
   gender, 82
Client seniority, 49–52
Code of ethics, 15, 43, 55–56, 112, 116
Colleagues and employers, 111–118
   commission splits, 114
   embezzling, 128
   grievances, 118
   hiring practices, 115
   listings, 116
   price-fixing, 114–115
   submitting offers, 120
   terminating employment, 119, 121
Commission splits, 113, 117
Complaints against practitioners, 2
Comprehensive Environmental
    Response, Compensation and
    Liability Act (CERCLA), 99
Condominiums, 86
Conscience, 35, 36, 42, 43, 64
Crime, 40–45, 95–97
Culver v. Jaoudi, 67
Customers vs. clients, 62–63

Decision making, ethical, 52
   integrated model for, 41
   models for, 39–52
   rational model for, 50

Rotarian model for, 52
Defects, 94, 104–105
Department of Housing and Urban
    Development (HUD), 77
Disclosure,
    AIDS, 93, 95–98
    agency, 66, 68, 72–75
    "as is," 100
    buyers' credit, 73
    crime, 89
    design flaws, 73
    earnest money deposit, 73
    environmental hazards, 99–105
    family relationships, 74
    gifts, 126
    latent defects, 94
    lead-based paint, 102–103
    limitation of expertise, 126
    market analysis, 74
    material defects, 93
    multiple offers, 114, 120–121
    murder–suicide, 40–45, 96, 97–98
    price of listing, 72
    radon gas, 101–102
    and RESPA, 126
    seller's responsibility, 103
    stigmatized properties, 93–98
Discrimination, 79–82
Dual agency,
    brokerage, 64–65
    legal, 65
    illegal, 65

Earnest money deposit, 73
Edina Realty, 65
Education,
    continuing, 2–3,
    courses, 117
    need for, 2, 127–128
Electromagnetic fields (EMFs), 2, 37
Embezzling, 128
End-results ethics, 28–29, 42
Environmental hazards, 99–110
Environmental Protection Agency
    (EPA), 99–100
Escrow monies, 123

Ethical decision making, guidelines,
    27, 44
    Integrated Model, 41–48
    Kew Gardens Principle, 45–48
    Rational Model of Ethical Analysis,
        49–52
    Rotarian model, 52
Ethical dilemmas, 4
    characteristics of, 8
Ethics,
    and agency, 61–75
    definition, 15–20
    and the law, 57–61
    myths, 3–5
    personal, 15–16
    programs, 3
    tests for, 38

Facilitation, 65
Fair Housing Act, 77
Fair housing, 77–82
    and AIDS, 93, 95–96, 98
    and crime, 89
    and Department of Housing and
        Urban Development (HUD), 77
Fiduciary responsibility, 61–63, 67

Genovese, Kitty, 45
Gifts, 126
Golden Rule, The, 6

Haunted house, 95
Hazardous materials disclosure
    form, 100
Hazards, environmental, 99–110
    disclosure of, 104
    lead-based paint, 102
    radon gas, 101–102
Heinz's Dilemma, 20
Hiring practices, 115

Inspections, 107–110
*Integrated Model for Ethical Decision
    Making,* 41, 48

Kanka, Megan, 48
Kant, Immanuel, 27, 31
Kew Gardens Principle, 45–48
Kohlberg, Lawrence, 19–23

Latent defects, 94
Lead-based paint, 2, 102–103
Listings, 116

Market analysis, 74
Material defects, 104–105, 109
Megan's Law, 48
Moral,
    competence, 3
    leadership, 13
    reasoning, 19–25
    relativism, 3
Moral development,
    sources of, 12–14
    stages of, 21–24
Multiple offers, 114, 120–121
Murder–suicide, 40–45, 96, 97, 98
Myths regarding ethics, 3–5

National Association of REALTORS®
    (NAR), 32, 55–56
    Code of Ethics, 55–56, 112
    *Code of Ethics and Arbitration
    Manual,* 113

Offers, 114, 120–121

Physical defects, 104–105
Practitioners,
    and the community, 123–126
    and demographic change, 3
    and politics, 125, 126–127
    and social change, 2–3
    and technological change, 2–3
Price fixing, 114–115
Principles,
    definition, 7–8
    and values, 9
Procuring cause, 113
Professional practice standards, 57–58

Profession, definition of, 56–57

Racial discrimination, 79–80, 81
Radon, 2, 101–102
Rational Model of Ethical Analysis,
    49–52
Real estate as a profession, 56–57
Reasonable person standard, 58–59
Reasoning, moral, 19–25
RESPA, 124
Resource Conservation and Recovery
    Act (RCRA), 99
Rotarian model of ethical decision
    making, 52
Rousseau, Jean Jacques, 28
Rule or law ethics, 31–32, 42

Seller,
    brokerage, 63
    responsibilities, 103–104
Single agency brokerage, 64
Social contract ethics, 32–35, 42
Solms, Christian and Melissa, 102
Stages of moral development, 21–24
Stigmatized properties, 93–98
    and AIDS, 95–98
Stuart, Charles, 94
Subagency, 63
Superfund, 99

Terminating employment, 119, 121
Thiroux, Jacques, 39
Transaction brokerage, 65
Transformational ethics, 35–37, 42

Utilitarianism, 28

Values,
    auction, 9–10
    definition, 7, 9
    and ethics, 15–17
    and principles, 7–9
    sources of, 12–14

Websites, 126